DA

THE ECOLOGY AND BEHAVIOR OF THE
LEWIS WOODPECKER (ASYNDESMUS LEWIS)

THE ECOLOGY AND BEHAVIOR OF THE LEWIS WOODPECKER (ASYNDESMUS LEWIS)

BY
CARL E. BOCK

UNIVERSITY OF CALIFORNIA PRESS
BERKELEY · LOS ANGELES · LONDON
1970

UNIVERSITY OF CALIFORNIA PUBLICATIONS IN ZOOLOGY
ADVISORY EDITORS: G. A. BARTHOLOMEW, J. H. CONNELL, JOHN DAVIS, C. R. GOLDMAN,
CADET HAND, K. S. NORRIS

Volume 92

Approved for publication October 17, 1969
Issued June 25, 1970
Price $3.00

UNIVERSITY OF CALIFORNIA PRESS
BERKELEY AND LOS ANGELES
CALIFORNIA

◇

UNIVERSITY OF CALIFORNIA PRESS, LTD.
LONDON, ENGLAND

ISBN: 0-520-09351-8
LIBRARY OF CONGRESS CATALOG CARD No. 73-629110

© 1970 BY THE REGENTS OF THE UNIVERSITY OF CALIFORNIA
PRINTED IN THE UNITED STATES OF AMERICA

CONTENTS

Introduction	1
Acknowledgments	2
Habit and Distribution	2
General distribution	2
Habitat preference—breeding season	4
Habitat preference—winter season	8
Analysis of distribution	9
Discussion	14
Migration and Opportunism	14
Introduction	14
Patterns of migration	15
Type of migratory flight	16
Timing of migration	17
Fall nomadism	20
Opportunism	21
Feeding Ecology and Behavior	23
Introduction	23
Structural adaptations	24
Sexual dimorphism	28
Feeding behavior	29
Summary of feeding ecology	39
Comparison with other woodpeckers	40
The ecology of acorn storage	43
Competition	46
Introduction	46
Winter territoriality	49
Evidence for physical displacement between Lewis and acorn woodpeckers	56
The problem of coexistence of acorn and Lewis woodpeckers	58
Analysis of interactions	59
Breeding Behavior	63
Vocalizations and displays	64
Timing of breeding	67
Pairing and nest sites	68
Incubation	71
Nestling period	72
Association of young with adults, and post-juvenile molt	75
Possible Evolution and Relationships	76
Summary	80
Literature Cited	83
Plates	93

THE ECOLOGY AND BEHAVIOR OF THE LEWIS WOODPECKER (ASYNDESMUS LEWIS)

BY

CARL E. BOCK

(A contribution from the Museum of Vertebrate Zoology
of the University of California)

INTRODUCTION

ON 20 JULY, 1805, Captain Meriwether Lewis wrote of seeing a strange woodpecker "as black as a crow" near the present site of Helena, Montana. In May of 1806 the Lewis and Clark party collected several specimens of the "black woodpecker" near Kamiah, Idaho; subsequently these were examined by the pioneer American ornithologist, Alexander Wilson, who gave the species the vernacular name of its discoverer. Wilson (1831:169) described the Lewis woodpecker (*Asyndesmus lewis*) as follows:

> The length was ... eleven inches and a half; the back, wings, and tail were black, with a strong gloss of green; upper part of the head, the same; front, chin, and cheeks, beyond the eyes, a dark rich red; round the neck passes a broad collar of white, which spreads over the breast, and looks as if the fibres of the feathers had been silvered; these feathers are also of a particular structure, the fibres being separate, and of a hair-like texture; belly, deep vermilion, and of the same strong hair-like feathers, intermixed with silvery ones; vent, black; legs and feet, dusky, inclining to greenish blue; bill, dark horn colour.

All that need be added to this description is that the sexes are very nearly identical, some females appearing slightly less strikingly colored than the males, and that young birds show little or no development of the silver collar or red face and belly, being a drab gray beneath for their first few months. There are no recognized subspecies.

In addition to its striking coloration, *Asyndesmus* is the most specialized of North American woodpeckers in the development of flycatching behavior and a unique slow, almost soaring, flight pattern related to this type of foraging. Although no major investigations of the Lewis woodpecker have been undertaken (except one unpublished study in Utah by R. B. Snow), because of its conspicuous habits there is a large amount of natural history information diluted in the writings of both amateur and professional ornithologists. Along with conducting my own field studies I have attempted to distill pertinent data from these published observations in an effort to present an overall picture of the Lewis woodpecker's ecology and behavior.

Asyndesmus lewis is an opportunistic species, feeding in spring and summer upon locally abundant insect populations, berries, and fruits, and in winter upon acorns which are stored in the fall. In California it is involved in an intense and unusual competition with a related species, the acorn woodpecker (*Melanerpes formicivorus*), which also stores acorns. It is hoped that the information presented will add to an understanding of opportunism and interspecific competition, two phenomena of interest to ecologists and which the Lewis woodpecker shows well.

I have divided this paper into sections related to various ecological and behavioral problems—feeding, functional anatomy, competition, nesting, and the like. However, it is important to remember that all autecological investigations basically are studies in adaptation and that the Lewis woodpecker did not evolve in sections but as a genetic whole. Therefore I have endeavored to show how the various aspects of its natural history combine to form an adaptive unit.

Field work for the project was carried out exclusively in California. I studied a breeding population at Boca Reservoir, Nevada County, during the summers of 1965 through 1968, a nesting population in the San Antonio Valley, Santa Clara County, in the spring of 1967, and winter populations in a variety of localities in lowland central California: the Capay Valley, Solano County, in 1967–68; the Old River, San Joaquin County, in 1964–65; the Livermore Valley, Alameda County, in 1966–67 and 67–68; and on Mount Hamilton, Santa Clara County, in 1965–66. Approximately 600 hours of actual observation time, on 152 days, were involved.

ACKNOWLEDGMENTS

Support during the course of this investigation came from a National Science Foundation Graduate Fellowship. Dr. A. Starker Leopold and Mr. Vernon M. Hawthorne made available all facilities of the Sagehen Creek Field Station, without which the research in the Sierra Nevada would have been impossible. A number of persons assisted in field work and participated in helpful discussions of the project—particularly Dr. Peter L. Ames, William Arvey, Brian M. Fitzgerald, Dr. Ned K. Johnson, and Vernon M. Hawthorne. Drs. Herbert G. Baker and Oliver P. Pearson read the manuscript and offered helpful criticisms and suggestions. Gene M. Christman provided advice and assistance in the preparation of illustrative material. I am grateful to my wife, Jane, for applying to the project her talents as a plant ecologist and photographer, as well as her endurance as a typist.

I am indebted to the late Dr. Alden H. Miller, whose patient guidance was invaluable during the initiation of the study. Finally, it is a pleasure to acknowledge the excellent counsel, stimulation, and editorial skills of Dr. John Davis.

HABITAT AND DISTRIBUTION

General Distribution

According to the American Ornithologists' Union Checklist (1957), the Lewis woodpecker:

Breeds from southern British Columbia, including Vancouver Island, western Alberta (Jasper Park), Montana (Lewiston, Billings), and southwestern South Dakota to southern California (Kern County), central Arizona, and southern New Mexico, east to northwestern Nebraska and eastern Colorado.

Winters regularly from northern Oregon (Portland, The Dalles), occasionally from southern British Columbia (southern Vancouver Island and Okanagan Valley), south to northern Baja California, northern Sonora, and southern Arizona, and from central Colorado and south central Nebraska to southern New Mexico and western Texas. *Casual* in Saskatchewan, Manitoba, northwestern Iowa, eastern Kansas, and Oklahoma. Accidental in Illinois and Rhode Island.

Figure 1 shows this distribution in detail, based upon 642 specific breeding or wintering localities taken from published literature references, and field notes

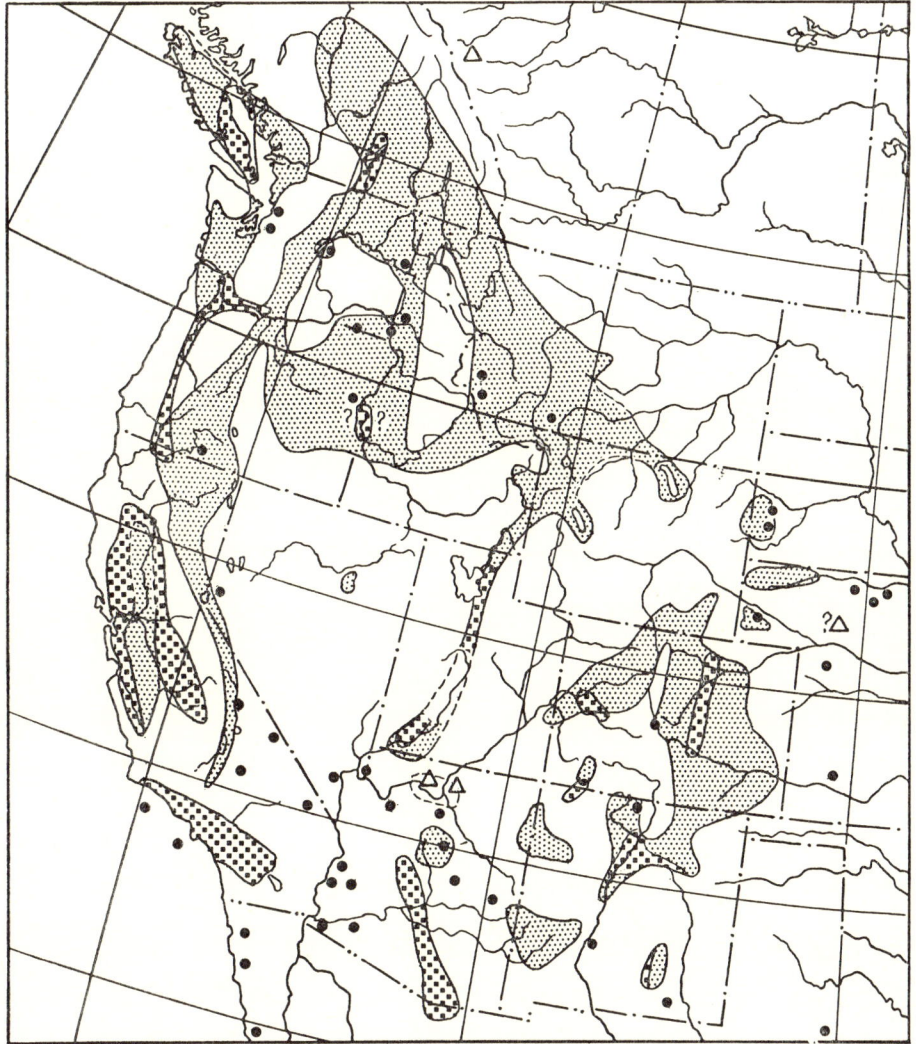

Fig. 1. Distribution of the Lewis woodpecker. Heavy stipple represents winter range; light stipple indicates breeding areas; dots are occasional winter records, while triangles signify possible breeding sites. The winter habitat in east-central Colorado is also nesting habitat. The breeding area in central California is part of a more extensive winter range.

and specimens in the Museum of Vertebrate Zoology. It does not include records of birds which could be considered migrants.

Status.—*Asyndesmus* can be sporadic in occurrence on breeding and wintering grounds; for this reason it seemed desirable to distinguish between areas occupied with some regularity and those used only rarely. The distinction is somewhat arbitrary, but I have classified areas as "occasional" (fig. 1) only if the number of individuals per record was small and if the birds were observed there on only one or two occasions. For example, *Audubon Field Notes* (1961) reported that two Lewis woodpeckers wintered near Dateland, Arizona, in 1961; this is represented on the map as "occasional." On the other hand, H. W. Henshaw (in Wheeler, 1875) found a group of about 100 birds wintering near Tularosa, New Mexico. Although there have been no other winter records published for this area, the large number seen by Henshaw suggests that it is good habitat and should be considered a "regular" wintering ground.

Another problem is that *Asyndesmus* tends to wander in fall. Some flocks or individuals may not settle permanently until late October or early November. Thus many "winter" records, especially in western Arizona and southeastern California (H. Brown, 1902; Robertson, 1935; Gilman, 1936) may refer only to transient birds.

Distributional limits.—Regarding southern limits, the status of the Lewis woodpecker in Baja California is uncertain. Grinnell and Lamb (1927) observed it in winter at San José and in the Guadalupe Valley. Huey (1931) found it at Cataviña in October. It probably is only a rare winter visitor in the northern part of Mexico proper (Miller et al., 1957).

Asyndesmus is rare east of New Mexico, Colorado, and westernmost South Dakota and Nebraska. Although Tout (1947) reports a possible breeding record in central Nebraska, and Swenk et al. (1945) list the Lewis woodpecker as wintering in this area, there have been no similar records in *Audubon Field Notes* for the past twenty years. Johnston (1960) described the species as a rare resident in southwestern Kansas, but now considers this unlikely (Johnston, personal communication).

Finally, there are few records anywhere north or east of southern British Columbia (Taverner, 1926; Munro and Cowan, 1947).

To summarize, *Asyndesmus* is found regularly from the plains of Colorado west to the Pacific, and from southern British Columbia to northernmost Mexico. The details of distribution within this broad area can best be explained by examining the habitats occupied.

HABITAT PREFERENCE—BREEDING SEASON

Lewis woodpeckers do not excavate into trees for insect larvae as do other woodpeckers, but feed extensively upon adult emergent insects in the manner of a swallow, flycatcher, or bluebird. They typically make prolonged sallies in pursuit of flying insects, usually initiated from prominent hawking perches. They will also drop from these perches into brush or grass for terrestrial insects. Related to these methods of foraging, one nearly universal characteristic of their breeding habitat is that of openness. Some trees are necessary for nesting and as hawking perches, but a dense coniferous forest or a woodland with closed canopy would restrict vision and aerial maneuvers and eliminate the brush or grass understory which supports important insect prey populations (see "Feeding Ecology and Behavior").

Table 1 summarizes specific literature records, personal observations, and unpublished field data which mention *Asyndesmus* habitats. This may not represent a random sample, as oak woodland and riparian situations generally are more accessible to observers than are coniferous forests. Nevertheless the data do give an indication of the preferred habitat types.

Open ponderosa pine forest.—Park-like ponderosa (*Pinus ponderosa* Dougl.) or "yellow" pine forest (pl. 1,*a*) probably is the major breeding habitat of the Lewis woodpecker. Ponderosa pine is widespread in the mountains of the West at intermediate altitudes and in areas of moderate precipitation. It grows in Arizona between 5,500 and 8,000 feet (1,677 to 2,439 meters) elevation (Kearney and Peebles, 1960), and in California between 2,000 and 9,000 feet (610 to 2,744 meters) altitude (Munz, 1959). To the north elevations decrease; in British Columbia ponderosa pine is common in the "Dry Forest Biotic Area" of Munro and Cowan (1947), between 1,000 and 3,000 feet (305 to 915 meters). It does not

TABLE 1
NUMBERS OF REFERENCES TO *Asyndesmus* HABITAT*

Habitat	Breeding season	Winter
Ponderosa pine	39 (30.5%)	0
Logged-burned forest	26 (20.3%)	0
Piñon-juniper	3 (2.3%)	1 (1.2%)
Open riparian woodland	40 (31.3%)	19 (22.6%)
Oak woodland	15 (11.7%)	48 (57.1%)
Orchards	5 (3.9%)	15 (17.9%)
Cornfields	0	1 (1.2%)
Total number of entries	128 (100%)	84 (100%)
Total number of references†	123	67

* Based upon published references, unpublished field data, and personal observation.
† The total numbers of references do not equal the totals of the entries because some references are for mixed habitat types such as cottonwood and oak, and these were tabulated under each.

occur along the humid north coast of California (Munz, 1959), and only sparsely west of the Cascade Range in Washington and Oregon (Jewett et al., 1953; Peck, 1961), where precipitation is high.

From 1965 to 1968 I studied a breeding population of *Asyndesmus* near Boca Reservoir, 1,700 meters, on the east slope of the Sierra Nevada, Nevada County, California. The birds nested in dead or partially decayed pines (pl. 1,*b*). Among the scattered trees was a scrub vegetation of common sagebrush (*Artemisia tridentata* Nutt.), golden currant (*Ribes aureum* Pursh.), bitter-brush (*Purshia tridentata* [Pursh.] DC), and rabbit-brush (*Chrysothamnus nauseosus* Britton). This brushy vegetation supported important insect prey populations and constituted a critical element of the habitat. The woodpeckers caught insects by flycatching out over the brush and also by dropping down and foraging in it. In this same region two pairs nested in dead pines adjacent to a wet meadow of *Carex* and *Juncus*. The birds made prolonged circling flights out over the meadow in pursuit of flying insects; they were often accompanied by tree swallows (*Iridoprocne bicolor*).

It is evident that the important feature of yellow pine forest is not the pines *per se*, but the openness of the habitat, and the nature of the understory and its insect fauna.

Logged or burned coniferous forest (pl. 2,*a*).—The logging or burning of a dense pine or fir forest creates a habitat structurally similar to open yellow pine, and the Lewis woodpecker is characteristic of such areas. Jewett et al. (1953:401) state that in Washington *Asyndesmus* "is seen more frequently in burned areas in the forest than in any other habitat." Dawson and Bowles (1909) likewise found it breeding west of the Cascade Range largely in cleared and burned regions. The dense Douglas fir forests (*Pseudotsuga menziesii* Franco) of western Washington would otherwise be unsuitable. Cowan (1940) and Pearse (1946) noted that *Asyndesmus* bred on Vancouver Island largely because of habitat created by logging operations. In their study of the woodpeckers of Lincoln County, Montana, the Weydemeyers (1928:345) found the Lewis woodpecker a regular resident of the Transition Zone, usually in yellow pine forest, but found that "in cut-over or burned woods it ranges to a higher elevation than in virgin forests."

In the first years after a fire, dead trees become infested with woodboring insects. Other woodpeckers, such as the three-toed (*Picoides* spp.) and hairy (*Dendrocopos villosus*) are well adapted for digging out woodborers (Burt, 1930; Spring, 1965), and may become common at this stage (Blackford, 1955; personal observations). Eventually dead trees begin to fall, and, should brush species invade, the area becomes good *Asyndesmus* habitat. Thus the Lewis woodpecker is characteristic of old burns rather than new ones.

In order to estimate at what ages burns are suitable for Lewis woodpeckers, I examined three different burns near the University of California Sagehen Creek Research Station, Nevada County, California. In 1960, the 39,000 acre Donner Ridge fire burned through much of the area. Most of the dead trees were still standing in 1968 (pl. 2,*b*). In four years of observation (1965 to 1968) only one adult and one juvenile were seen on this burn, moving quickly through it together.

In 1946, a fire burned on the east side of Boca Reservoir. I observed Lewis woodpeckers breeding here from 1965 to 1968; the birds nested in the remaining scattered dead snags (pl. 2,*a*). Brushy vegetation was much more highly developed here than anywhere in the area of the Donner Ridge fire, and consisted of tobacco brush (*Ceanothus velutinus* Dougl. ex Hook.), bitter-brush, golden currant, and greenleaf manzanita (*Arctostaphylos patula* Greene).

The north slope at the head of the Sagehen Creek Basin was burned many years ago, probably in the 1920's (pl. 3,*a*). It is now a nearly impenetrable stand of tobacco brush and greenleaf manzanita. Only a few stumps remain of the original forest. A small group of post-breeding *Asyndesmus* visited this old burn in August, 1966. However, I found no birds nesting here from 1965 to 1968. No one has recorded the species breeding in the Sagehen Basin, although many observers have collected and done field work here since the mid-1950's. A shortage of nest-sites and possibly an insufficient variety of insects in the more uniform brushfields may have caused this area to become unsuitable.

Burned areas, in their process of decay and revegetation, are potential *Asyndesmus* breeding habitat for only a part of the cycle. The Donner Ridge burn is now seven years old and probably will not be a good area for several more seasons. The Boca fire area has definitely supported a breeding population in its 19th through 22nd years, and for an unknown number of years previously. The Sagehen burn apparently has been unused at least since its 30th year.

Not all burned or logged coniferous forests revert to brushfields. Much of the Donner Ridge burn appears to be coming back as ponderosa pine, and such dense second growth forest is the antithesis of *Asyndesmus* habitat. Similarly, the Lewis woodpecker was a common nesting species at Glenbrook, Lake Tahoe, Nevada, following logging operations in the late 1800's (Linsdale, 1936a). This area is now dense second growth ponderosa pine and white fir (*Abies concolor* Lindl.), and the Lewis woodpecker is absent there (N. K. Johnson, MS).

Piñon-juniper woodland.—Merriam (1890) found Lewis woodpeckers breeding in the piñon-juniper belt between 6,000 and 7,000 feet (1,830 to 2,134 meters) in the San Francisco Mountains of Arizona. Bendire (1895) describes the species as nesting in junipers, but gives no specific localities. L. H. Miller (1904) found birds nesting in junipers as well as pines in the John Day region of Oregon. I have found no other records, and it would appear that this habitat is infrequently occupied (table 1). Although piñon-juniper woodland is open, it occurs in lower and drier areas than yellow pine (Odum, 1959) and probably does not support insects in the abundance or variety of the latter.

Open riparian woodland (pl. 3,b).—At lower elevations, riparian woodland (particularly cottonwood) replaces coniferous forest as the main *Asyndesmus* breeding habitat (table 1). For example, N. K. Johnson (MS) found Lewis woodpeckers breeding in open yellow pine between 5,000 and 6,000 feet (1,525 to 1,830 meters) on the east slope of the Carson Range in western Nevada; while along the base of this range, from 4,000 to 5,100 feet (1,220 to 1,550 meters), they nested in Fremont cottonwoods (*Populus fremontii* Wats.). Similarly, Lewis woodpeckers breed in pine forest along the Front Range of the Rocky Mountains in Colorado, but frequent cottonwoods on the plains to the east (Bailey and Niedrach, 1965; Niedrach, personal communication).

Cottonwoods are good habitat for a number of reasons. First, groves usually are open. Near Genoa, Douglas County, Nevada, I watched birds making prolonged hawking flights out over the meadows and marshlands between isolated stands of Fremont cottonwoods (pl. 3,b). The larger trees were used as hawking perches.

Second, because of changing stream and riverbeds there usually are a number of dead trees in a given area which afford nest and roost sites. Since Lewis woodpeckers are not specialized for chiseling into wood for food, nest construction is more difficult than for other woodpeckers; they seem to prefer decayed wood.

Finally, the vegetation in riparian areas is more varied and lush than in drier uplands. It follows that insects would also be more numerous, both in number and kind. This is particularly the case in the West because of the usual summer drought.

Asyndesmus will nest in other riparian vegetation similar to cottonwood. In central Utah, R. B. Snow (MS) found birds nesting "in poplar, black willow, cottonwood, and boxelder trees." In central California, the Lewis woodpecker nests in western sycamore (*Platanus racemosa* Nutt.) as well as cottonwood (Hoffmann, 1927; Bolander, 1930; Gladding, 1942; personal observations). Physically there is little difference between the two habitats. *Platanus* grows along streams and usually is rather well spaced. Peattie (1953:596) observed that "because Sycamores are so often hollow, Gila and Lewis and Arizona woodpeckers all delight to nest in it."

Oak woodland (pls. 4,*a* and 4,*b*).—Although this is primarily winter habitat, Lewis woodpeckers will nest in oak (*Quercus*) woodland, usually along watercourses or in open, more savannah-like areas. I studied a resident population in the oak savannah of the San Antonio Valley, Santa Clara County, California, from January, 1967, to May, 1968. Pairs nested in dead trees or the hollow limbs of living trees; they foraged largely in and over grassland openings in the woods.

In the Central Valley of California, Belding (1878:430) found the Lewis woodpecker to be "a common resident of Stockton and Marysville, and . . . more numerous in the valleys than in the foothills." He (op. cit.: 389) described the country around Stockton as "sparsely timbered, though the principal water-courses are marked by a narrow strip of oaks and willows." From this it seems that the birds were visiting the riparian valley oaks (*Quercus lobata* Neé.), but were not abundant in the more continuous woodlands of the surrounding foothills.

In Yakima County, Washington, W. Sturman (personal communication) found a sizable population breeding in a dense grove of Garry oaks (*Quercus garryana* Dougl.). However, the birds actually were foraging outside the grove in the surrounding sage and cultivated lands.

There are several possible reasons why *Asyndesmus* might not breed more often in oak woodland. First, much of it simply is too dense. Another possibility already discussed is that insects are not available in sufficient numbers for breeding except near water. Of the 15 nesting localities in oak woodland listed in table 1, 7 are along riverbanks. These, taken with the 40 records from cottonwoods, sycamores, and the like, suggest that a riparian situation is the only one regularly suitable for nesting at lower elevations.

A third reason why oaks may be less suitable for nesting is that their wood is relatively hard. Finally, there is evidence to suggest that interspecific competition may be more intense in oak woodland than elsewhere (see "Competition").

Orchards (pl. 5,*a*).—Although orchards usually are winter habitat, Lewis woodpeckers occasionally will breed in oaks or riparian trees near an orchard and feed upon the fruits or nuts. This is not only a unique habitat, but also constitutes a major change in diet during the breeding season. I have observed birds nesting in sycamores near Livermore, Alameda County, California, and feeding green almonds from the surrounding orchards to their nestlings. A single pair nesting in a dead oak near Tracy, San Joaquin County, California, also fed almonds to their young (pl. 4,*b*). Snow (MS) found *Asyndesmus* nesting in farmland in north-central Utah; they not only took insects in the usual manner but also fed on a variety of soft fruits grown in the area.

HABITAT PREFERENCE—WINTER SEASON

In the fall Lewis woodpeckers move to oak woodland or commercial nut orchards where they harvest and store acorns or nuts in caches for the winter (pls. 5,*b* and 6,*a*). Since emergent insects are much less abundant then, this stored mast forms a critical proportion of the winter diet.

In the Central Valley of California many oaks have been removed while the number of orchards has greatly increased. The California almond crop was estimated at 15,000 tons in 1940 and 71,000 tons in 1965 (Reed, 1966). It is not surprising therefore that Lewis woodpeckers often have foresaken oaks for orchards. I have found that birds wintering today in the valley usually are associated with almond and walnut trees (pl. 6,a). They store nut meats in the checked bark of oaks, or, more often, in the desiccation cracks of old power poles (pl. 6,b).

Paul Baldwin (personal communication) discovered birds near Fort Collins, Colorado, doing "nearly all their feeding in the open top of a silo where they could get corn." In this case the storing had been done for them.

Over 95 percent of the winter habitat records are from oak woodland or various agricultural equivalents (table 1), indicating the importance of stored foods in winter. However, oak woodland is more regularly occupied where winters are mild, suggesting that insect abundance also is important even when mast is available.

The one area where the Lewis woodpecker may winter without a store of mast is in the deserts of southwestern Arizona and southeastern California (fig. 1). *Audubon Field Notes* records (Yuma, Parker, Weeden, Dateland) are numerous enough to suggest that birds may winter in Yuma County, Arizona, at least occasionally. Though *Quercus* is absent (Kearney and Peebles, 1960), Yuma County does produce about one fifth of the state's pecans (*U. S. Agric. Census,* 1964), and the birds might be using pecan meat as stored food. Miller and Stebbins (1964) reported birds occasionally wintering in cottonwoods around springs in the Joshua Tree National Monument, California. However, scrub oak (*Quercus dumosa* Nutt.) grows in the Monument (Miller and Stebbins, op. cit.) and may provide mast. More field work is needed to determine to what degree *Asyndesmus* may or may not winter without mast in the Southwest.

I have found no definite records of Lewis woodpeckers feeding upon piñon nuts, although D. H. Johnson et al. (1948) discovered a small flock in winter in piñon-juniper habitat in the Providence Mountains of California.

ANALYSIS OF DISTRIBUTION

With this outline of habitat preferences in mind, it is now possible to give some interpretation to the rather complex distribution shown in figure 1. This should be considered a minimum range map since more field work will undoubtedly expand the distribution. *Asyndesmus* basically is an opportunistic species, and thus a definitive distribution map will never be possible.

Dashed lines indicate areas of uncertainty, where data either are limited or lacking. *Asyndesmus* distribution is roughly horseshoe-shaped, beginning in the continuous forests of southern British Columbia and the northwestern United States, and continuing down both the coastal and central mountain chains. In discussing distribution, I have arbitrarily begun in southern California, moved north and then east and finally south to Arizona and New Mexico.

Winter.—Along the Pacific Coast, the major *Asyndesmus* wintering grounds are in central and southern California (fig. 1). The abundance and variety of oaks and the relatively mild, snow-free winters make these areas highly suitable. Lewis woodpeckers are common in winter in southern California from Santa Barbara (Streator, 1886) southeast to San Diego County (Marsden, 1907), and at least occasionally into Baja California (Grinnell and Lamb, 1927; Huey, 1931). They also winter widely in northern California, from the foothills of the Sierra Nevada and Cascade Range (Welch, 1899; Grinnell et al., 1930) west through the remainder of the state, except for the humid region along the north coast, the relatively barren southern end of the Central Valley, and the southern foothills of the Sierra Nevada and South Coast Range. There are winter records south to Fresno County in the valley (Hubbard, 1941), and winter birds have been recorded to Paso Robles, San Luis Obispo County, in the South Coast Range (*Audubon Field Notes,* 1954). Oaks are scarce today in the floor of the valley itself, but extensive almond orchards provide a good substitute.

According to Peck (1961), *Quercus* grows in the valleys of the Rogue, Umpqua, Willamette, and Columbia river systems in Oregon (in the latter, as far east as the Deschutes tributary). *Asyndesmus* winter range follows this closely (fig. 1). Gabrielson and Jewett (1940:375) state that the Lewis woodpecker "winters more or less regularly in Columbia, Snake, John Day, and Willamette valleys and more commonly in Umpqua and Rogue river valleys." Since *Quercus* does not occur in the John Day and Snake River areas, and I have found no other records of the species wintering there, it seems likely that the birds seen by Gabrielson and Jewett were only vagrants or fall migrants.

It is noteworthy that Gabrielson and Jewett (op. cit.) found the Lewis woodpecker to be more abundant in the Rogue and Umpqua river regions than elsewhere. In these two valleys and in the southern Willamette Valley a variety of oaks reach their northern limits of distribution (Peck, 1961); beyond, only the Garry oak occurs. Oak species diversity probably insures a more regular acorn supply and would provide better winter habitat. The acorn woodpecker (*Melanerpes formicivorus*), which is a resident of oak woodland and highly dependent upon acorns (Ritter, 1938), likewise is common only as far north as the southern end of the Willamette Valley (Gabrielson and Jewett, 1940).

The Lewis woodpecker rarely winters in Washington (Jewett et al., 1953), although the Garry oak occurs in lowlands of the western part of the state (Hitchcock et al., 1964). However, it apparently winters with some regularity in Garry oaks on the southern end of Vancouver Island, British Columbia (Munro and Cowan, 1947).

Occasional records in the Okanagan Valley present a problem. There are no oaks in this part of British Columbia, but there is a large apple-growing industry (Cowan, personal communication). Such soft fruits could not be stored, but might be available most of the winter. This assumes that a sufficient amount of fruit is left on the tree or on the ground after the fall harvest. *Audubon Field Notes* has published records of Lewis woodpeckers wintering near Wenatchee, Washington, where there are no oaks. According to Wm. G. Baldwin, M.D. (personal communication) these birds feed on apples and other fruit left on the trees throughout the winter.

Neff (1928) found that in the fall Lewis woodpeckers invaded apple orchards in the Rogue River Valley, but that they moved into oaks to winter. There are a number of similar observations, suggesting that in most cases soft fruit orchards are not used as permanent wintering areas.

There are occasional reports in *Audubon Field Notes* of Lewis woodpeckers wintering in Montana, Idaho, eastern Oregon, and eastern Washington; but these are only accidental records—usually of one or two birds. Similarly, the species is only a rare resident of the Black Hills, South Dakota (Pettingill and Whitney, 1965). Although the bur oak (*Quercus macrocarpa* A. Michaux) grows here (Peattie, 1953), severe winters probably drive most birds south. The Lewis woodpecker appears to be rare in winter in Nebraska; there has only been one individual reported in *Audubon Field Notes* in the last twenty years (Christmas—Scott's Bluff). Bruner et al. (1904) recorded *Asyndesmus* in winter in Brown and Cherry counties, Nebraska. According to Swenk et al. (1945), it winters east to Brown and Adams counties. Tout (1947) reported a bird in January from Lincoln County. None of these records mentions oaks, although the bur oak would be present (Weaver, 1965).

Gambel oaks (*Quercus gambelii* Nutt.) occur in the foothills of the Front Range in Colorado (Harrington, 1964); *Asyndesmus* frequently winters here from Fort Collins to Pueblo (Bailey and Niedrach, 1965; numerous *Audubon Field Notes* records) probably utilizing both acorns and corn. Brewster (1898) described *Asyndesmus* storing acorns near Denver in what apparently is the first published record of the storing process. *Audubon Field Notes* has published records of wintering Lewis woodpeckers from Grand Junction, Paonia, and Hotchkiss in western Colorado. There also are several Christmas Count records from Durango, La Plata County, in the southern part of the state. Although none of these specifically mentions oaks or acorns, the Gambel oak occurs in these areas (Harrington, 1964) and its acorns are undoubtedly used.

R. B. Snow (MS) studied the Lewis woodpecker in the Salt Lake region of Utah. He found that the birds were nearly resident, wintering in the western foothills and canyon mouths of the Wasatch Mountains and moving down to the valley floor to breed. Snow states: "Usually within a short distance of the creek bottoms and on the higher foothills are found the Gambel Oaks. These trees, some of whose limbs are often dead, and the acorn crop of the oaks, make ideal winter grounds for the Lewis Woodpecker. The dead limbs are all dry and contain many desiccation cracks for the storage of acorns." There are *Asyndesmus* winter records as far north as Ogden and south to Washington County. An apparent gap in the central part of the state probably reflects a lack of extensive field work, as oak-cottonwood habitat is continuous along the Wasatch Mountains (W. H. Behle, personal communication).

Wintering *Asyndesmus* seem strangely local in New Mexico and Arizona. I have recorded available published records in figure 1, but the range is not explicable in terms of widespread oak distribution. This also is true of western Colorado. The acorn woodpecker is found widely in the oak woodlands of New Mexico and Arizona (F. M. Bailey, 1928; Phillips et al., 1964), yet Lewis woodpeckers have not been recorded in most of these areas. This is in sharp contrast to California and Oregon, where the ranges of the two are virtually identical. One possible explanation involves the milder winter climate of the Pacific Coast. The storage habit is highly developed in the acorn woodpecker (Ritter, 1938); thus it probably can rely to a greater degree upon cached acorns, while *Asyndesmus* winters in areas where numbers of emergent insects would also be available. As discussed earlier, Lewis woodpeckers may winter in the deserts of the Southwest with little or no mast available. The acorn woodpecker is only a rare vagrant in this area, indicating again its more complete dependence on oaks. According to F. M. Bailey (1928), in New Mexico the acorn woodpecker is typical of areas where yellow pine and oaks intergrade. Winters may be too severe here for *Asyndesmus*. Bailey (op. cit.) reports a flock of Lewis woodpeckers near Chama, Rio Arriba County, which was present until mid-December, but which disappeared following a heavy snowstorm.

As in New Mexico, oaks (Kearney and Peebles, 1960) and acorn woodpeckers are more widespread in Arizona than wintering Lewis woodpeckers; there are *Melanerpes formicivorus* records east along the the Mogollon Rim, north to the Grand Canyon, and northeast to Apache County. *Asyndesmus* seems to be more abundant in the low southern and western part of the range of *Quercus*, suggesting again the importance of milder winters. Most recent *Audubon Field Notes* records are from Nogales north through Tucson, Phoenix, and Prescott. This may be an artifact associated with these centers of population, but I have tentatively indicated this as regular winter range (fig. 1). The Phoenix area (Pinal and Maricopa counties) produces nearly one half of Arizona's pecans (*U. S. Agric. Census*, 1964). Lewis woodpeckers probably are attracted to these orchards.

Breeding season.—In California, the Lewis woodpecker breeds mainly in open ponderosa pine, burns, and logged areas on the eastern slopes of the Sierra Nevada and Cascade Range (e.g.: Grinnell and Storer, 1924; Grinnell et al., 1930). Along the east base of the Sierra Nevada it breeds in Fremont cottonwoods. I have found no definite breeding records for the western slopes, where forests more often are dense. The southernmost definite breeding locality is Taylor Meadow, 7,000 feet (2,135 meters), Tulare County (Grinnell, MS). However, birds were seen in June near Tejon Pass, Ventura County by Fisher (1893) and by Lamb and Howell (1913). I have tentatively included this area in figure 1.

There are no breeding records for southern California. It is not altogether clear why this should be so; but the summer drought there (Dale, 1959) may be too extreme for adequate insect life.

In central California, the Lewis woodpecker breeds in the northern half of the Central Valley as far south as Stockton, San Joaquin County (Belding, 1890), and in the South Coast Range, from Livermore (personal observation) to northern San Luis Obispo County (Thompson, 1900).

It seems that *Asyndesmus* formerly may have been more widespread in the northern Central Valley than it is today. Ridgway (1874) found it an abundant breeding bird between Sacramento and Auburn in June and July, 1867. Belding (1890) listed it as a common resident of Stockton and Marysville. Townsend (1887:206) wrote: "It is a constant resident of the valleys and foothills." Presumably he was referring to the northernmost section of the valley in which he collected and explored. There apparently are no similar records since these, although in 1964 I discovered a single nest in a dead valley oak near Tracy, San Joaquin County. The riparian woodland bordering the Sacramento and San Joaquin River systems has been so reduced that Munz (1959) does not describe a riverine community such as discussed by Jepson (1911). Also, the original grasslands of the valley now are totally altered by agriculture. The combined effects of nest-site reduction and cultivation apparently have made this area much less suitable for breeding. Today Lewis woodpeckers breed west of the Sierra Nevada mainly in the South Coast Range. They commonly nest in sycamore and cottonwood, less often in oak (Thompson, 1900; Hoffmann, 1927; Bolander, 1930; Gladding, 1942; personal observation).

Gabrielson and Jewett (1940) list *Asyndesmus* as a summer resident in every part of Oregon. The species breeds in yellow pine, cottonwood, and occasionally in juniper along the more arid east side of the Cascades and in the mountains of northeastern Oregon (Bendire, 1895; Merrill, 1888; Jewett, 1909; Peck, 1911; Walker, 1917). *Asyndesmus* does not occur in the deserts of southeastern Oregon, nor are there records for the dense coniferous forests of the high Cascades or the coastal mountains, except for a logged portion of Tillamook County (Walker, 1924). Birds occasionally breed in oaks of the western lowlands (Bendire, 1895; Walker, 1917; Neff, 1928).

Jewett et al. (1953) divide the Transition Zone of Washington into a western humid region, dominated by Douglas fir, and an eastern semi-arid region, characterized by open ponderosa pine forests with an understory of sage, bitter-brush, currant, and the like. Black cottonwood (*Populus trichocarpa* T. & G.) grows in lowlands both east and west of the Cascade Range. *Asyndesmus* breeds in open ponderosa pines and cottonwoods east of the Cascades, except in the central desert area (Dawson, 1897; Snodgrass, 1903, 1904; Dice, 1921). Yocom (1945) found Lewis woodpeckers nesting in burned areas in the Selkirk Mountains of northeastern Washington. West of the Cascades, nesting occurs either in cottonwoods (Bendire, 1895; Dicks, 1932) or in logged and burned Douglas fir forest (Rathbun, 1902; Dawson and Bowles, 1909).

In British Columbia, Munro and Cowan (1947:139) describe the Lewis woodpecker as a "summer visitant of open forest and wooded roadsides in the southern half of the Province from the coast to the Rocky Mountains." *Asyndesmus* breeds most often in open ponderosa pine forest (Chapman, 1890; Rhoads, 1893; Johnstone, 1949). This is extensive in the interior valleys of southeastern British Columbia, in the "Dry Forest Biotic Area" of Munro and Cowan. Elsewhere, birds frequently nest in logged or burned regions (A. Brooks, 1917), including Vancouver Island (Cowan, 1940; Pearse, 1946).

Asyndesmus breeds widely in the northern Rocky Mountains, although I have found no records for much of the Bitterroot Range in northern and eastern Idaho (fig. 1). Hand (1941) found that across the panhandle of Idaho, in the St. Joe National Forest, the species bred in open timber on the lower slopes but did not nest at higher elevations to the east. It nests on the western and southern slopes of the Bitterrroot Range (Merriam, 1891; Hand, 1941), and east into Montana as far as Billings and Lewiston (Saunders, 1921). Nests have been recorded in ponderosa pine (Saunders, 1921; Weydemeyer & Weydemeyer, 1928), cottonwood (Saunders, 1911, 1914, 1921), burns (Silloway, 1901), and in logged areas (Burleigh, 1921) in the northern Rockies. Knight (1902) found Lewis woodpeckers breeding in the mountains of northwestern and southeastern Wyoming, and observed that they seemed most abundant in burned timber.

There are isolated breeding populations of the Lewis woodpecker in Nebraska and South Dakota. Pettingill and Whitney (1965) discuss a small population which nests in burns, open pine forest, and (at lower elevations) cottonwood, in the Black Hills of South Dakota. Bruner et al. (1904) and Swenk et al. (1945) note that the Lewis woodpecker breeds in the ponderosa pine forests of northwestern Nebraska.

In Colorado, *Pinus ponderosa* occurs down the Front Range of the Rocky Mountains and between 1,800 and 2,600 meters in western and central counties; cottonwoods occur both east and west of the central mountain chain (Harrington, 1964). The Lewis woodpecker breeds in the pines along the Front Range (Bailey and Niedrach, 1965), and in cottonwoods on the plains east nearly to Kansas (Niedrach, personal communication). They also nest west of the highest Rockies as far as the La Sal Mountains of eastern Utah (Rockwell, 1908; Warren, 1916; Snow, MS). Although breeding birds have been recorded from San Juan and La Plata counties (Drew, 1881; Gilman, 1907), I have found no specific records for the remainder of the San Juan Mountains in southwestern Colorado. This seems an unlikely gap and probably is an artifact.

Asyndesmus breeds in deciduous trees along the west base of the Wasatch Mountains in central Utah (Woodbury et al., 1949; Snow, MS). It is surprising that apparently there are no breeding records for the ponderosa pine forests of the Wasatch and Uinta mountains. I have not included these areas on the range map, but more field work might find the species there.

In New Mexico, *Asyndesmus* nests in pine forests in the mountainous portions of the state (Hunn, 1906; F. M. Bailey, 1928; J. S. Ligon, 1961), and occasionally in lowland riparian situations (Ligon, op cit.; Jensen, 1923). Lewis woodpeckers breed regularly in the ponderosa and piñon-juniper forests of the San Francisco Mountains in Arizona (Coues, 1874; Merriam, 1890; Phillips et al., 1964). There also are records from the mountains of northeastern Apache County (Woodbury and Russell, 1945). Elsewhere in Arizona the species is rare during the breeding season.

Discussion

It is possible to describe potential *Asyndesmus* breeding habitat in terms of nest sites and the physical structure suited to the species' methods of foraging. However, it is only a locally abundant breeding bird; the selection of one small area and the rejection of others within a broad habitat type most likely depends upon differences in insect abundance. The Lewis woodpecker clearly is an opportunistic species; there are records of birds responding to locust swarms and other insect outbreaks by tremendously increasing breeding densities. It follows that more subtle fluctuations in prey numbers will determine whether the Lewis woodpecker occurs in a given area at all. The subject of opportunism and the response to fluctuations in food supply will be discussed in the next section.

MIGRATION AND OPPORTUNISM

Introduction

In the fall, Lewis woodpeckers which have bred in open pine forest, old burns, or riparian cottonwood groves move to oak woodland or nut orchards where they rely upon stored mast (acorns, almonds, and the like) during the winter. These "migrations" from breeding to wintering grounds and back are irregular in their nature and extent for three reasons. First, while some birds nest far from oaks or orchards, others breed very near suitable winter habitat or may be permanent residents in it. Therefore the distances traveled by migrating birds differ strikingly. Second, Lewis woodpeckers often do not travel directly from breeding to wintering grounds but instead may form in late summer into nomadic flocks which move into the higher mountains or invade fruit orchards before proceeding to permanent winter areas. Lastly, *Asyndesmus* is highly opportunistic, nesting where insects are temporarily abundant and concentrating in winter where the year's acorn crop happens to be high. This means that migratory routes are not fixed, and that the occurrence of Lewis woodpeckers in both breeding and winter seasons is sporadic at any one locality. The general food requirements for nesting and wintering are constant, and thus also the habitat types for each, but the suitability of a particular area may vary from year to year. This section presents information, gathered largely from literature sources, documenting the migratory behavior and opportunism exhibited by the Lewis woodpecker.

Patterns of Migration

Although data on the migration routes of particular populations are scant, Lewis woodpeckers appear to move in the fall to the nearest suitable winter habitat. Snow (MS) found that birds which bred in agricultural lowlands at the western edge of the Wasatch Mountains in north-central Utah moved to Gambel oaks (*Quercus gambelii*), in the foothills of this range, to winter. His map indicates that the distances between summer and winter territories varied between 0.8 and 9.0 kilometers. Similarly, much of the movement to and away from the oaks along the Front Range in Colorado may involve very local movement only (fig. 1). Lewis woodpeckers breed in ponderosa pine (*Pinus ponderosa*) at slightly higher elevations and also in cottonwoods on the plains immediately to the east (Bailey and Niedrach, 1965). Cowan (1940) noted that birds breeding in logged-over parts of Vancouver Island generally departed in September, but that a few remained all winter, presumably in the Garry oaks (*Quercus garryana*) on the southern end of the island; he observed that winter temperatures were higher than in the late 1800's and suggested that this might account for the recent records of *Asyndesmus* wintering there. Pettingill and Whitney (1965) report that birds breeding in the Black Hills of South Dakota may winter locally at lower elevations in mild years.

In contrast to these local movements, Lewis woodpeckers which breed in such places as Idaho, Wyoming, and Montana must travel considerable distances to reach winter range. There is no conclusive evidence to indicate where these populations do go in the fall. They might move west to Oregon and California or southeast into Colorado, in addition to south into Utah and Arizona.

Asyndesmus apparently is not common in Arizona except for "flight years" (Phillips et al., 1964:71–2) when very large numbers of birds appear. H. Brown (1902) and Scott (1886) reported large flocks seen in the winter of 1884–85; in 1946–47 there was another major flight in western Arizona (Phillips et al., 1964). In 1948–49, *Audubon Field Notes* recorded the largest flight since 1884. Significantly, that winter was one of the most severe in recent history throughout all of the western and central United States. These large flights into Arizona may be caused by severe weather conditions in the northern parts of the species' range.

The winter population in southern California also varies considerably from year to year. *Audubon Field Notes* recorded 1950 and 1960 as good flight years, with the intervening nine years being rather poor. This variation probably relates to the abundance of the local acorn crop (see page 22) as well as weather conditions in the north. There is no conclusive evidence to indicate where populations which winter in the Los Angeles basin have bred.

The major breeding populations of the Lewis woodpecker in California occur along the east base of the Sierra Nevada and in the Cascade Range. Migrant records from the western slopes and foothills of the Sierra Nevada suggest that birds breeding to the east cross the mountains to winter in the oaks and orchards of the Central Valley, supporting the general rule that Lewis woodpeckers move to the closest suitable wintering area. Belding (1890) observed birds moving west over the Sierra Nevada crest, between 16 August and 7 September. Belding (1901) also saw a single bird being driven west from Donner Pass, Nevada County, by a late snowstorm on 15 May, 1898. Spring and fall migrants are common in the Yosemite region in the western Sierra Nevada (Grinnell and Storer, 1924). E. Michael (1932:4) observed thousands of birds moving through Yosemite Valley in the fall, "winging their way to winter feeding grounds."

Large populations regularly reported near Redding and Red Bluff by *Audubon Field Notes* provide evidence that breeding birds of the Cascade region move into this northern extension of the Sacramento Valley to winter. Smith (1941) in fact observed several thousand Lewis woodpeckers moving southward in September near the town of Mount Shasta, Siskiyou County, suggesting such a migratory route.

Asyndesmus of the Pacific Northwest apparently move southward and coastward in the winter. Except for small winter populations in British Columbia, birds nesting in this region must move into the lowland river valleys of western Oregon, or proceed south to the oak woodlands of northern California. Merrill (1888) noted that birds breeding in southern Oregon near Fort Klamath were joined by many flocks moving in from the north. All *Asyndesmus* left the area in September, presumably moving south to California or west to the Rogue River Valley. Jewett et al. (1953) recorded a large southward flight in mid-September near Lake Washington, King County, Washington. Jewett and Gabrielson (1929) report a similar migration near Portland on 14 September.

Type of Migratory Flight

Published observations of Lewis woodpeckers in migration are scarce. The most extensive account is that of Smith (1941) who carefully documented a large flight south through Siskiyou County, California, between 10 and 17 September, 1940. Smith observed (op. cit.:76):

During the half hour from 9:25 to 9:55 a.m., 1,018 birds, by actual count crossed over a fixed line, and many others undoubtedly escaped notice because of being too far away to be seen. Although at times only one or two individuals were in sight, on several occasions the numbers crossing the line were so great as to make it difficult to count them all. The speed of flight was typical of their manner on and about foraging grounds, and averaged about the same throughout the period of observation. Well over 5,000 birds must have passed within sight during that time. Some of the birds seemed tired, and took advantage of the proximity of several snags (relics of an old burn) to rest for a short time. Probably no one bird remained perched for more than a minute or two, and there were rarely more than two birds on a snag at any one time.

The line of flight was between Mt. Shasta and Black Butte (Wintoon Butte). At this point an extensive brush field of manzanita (*Arctostaphylos patula*), ceanothus, and other chaparral covered a fairly level area about two miles wide, at an average altitude of about 4,300 feet above sea level. The flight probably extended over the whole two-mile front. The woodpeckers flew at heights of from 10 feet above ground to those at which they were barely discernible.

The flight was quiet and no vocal sound was heard, although many birds passed within earshot. None of the birds was seen to feed, and they seemed indifferent to my movements, even when close by. Smaller flights passed over the same area on September 14 and 17. These later flocks flew by in groups of as many as 78 birds, but there were intervals of half an hour or more during which none was seen. Except for this difference in number, the three flights were all alike.

Adams (1941:119) discovered flights near Trimmer Springs, Fresno County, California, on 4 and 9 September, 1940, and observed: "There was no apparent formation in the mass flight of these woodpeckers. Instead, they passed over in straggly groups of two to fifteen individuals. Some of them flew within a few feet of each other and others flew as much as several hundred feet apart. All traveled in a relatively straight line and none was seen to stop. They flew at various altitudes, but none flew lower than an estimated 150 feet above the hilltops. Others were so high that they were almost out of sight."

The type of migratory flight shown by *Asyndesmus*—diurnal, rather slow, with birds occasionally straggling for a time—apparently is typical for migrant woodpeckers generally. Bent (1939) reports similar migratory behavior in *Dendrocopos villosus*, *Sphyrapicus varius*, *Colaptes auratus*, and *Centurus carolinus*. Helme (1882:107) observed this sort of migration in red-headed woodpeckers (*Melanerpes erythrocephalus*) moving through Long Island, and noticed that "many of them in their flight would alight for a few minutes in the orchards and corn fields to feed on the half ripened corn...."

Timing of Migration

Tables 2 and 3 are summaries of spring and fall migration dates for *Asyndesmus*. These data were obtained from a variety of references, particularly the spring and fall migration issues of *Audubon Field Notes*, Oberholser (1927), F. M. Bailey (1928), Munro and Cowan (1947), and Jewett et al. (1953). Other specific references are cited in the tables.

Since *Asyndesmus* migrate slowly, often lingering in particular localities, and do not make prolonged high altitude flights between breeding and wintering areas, it was often impossible to separate records of actual departures and arrivals from those of birds already leaving an area or still in the process of settling in another. Therefore, I have included all records of migrating birds in the data for the regions in which they were observed, with the result that the mean dates for migration shown in tables 2 and 3 represent an average time for movement from or into an area, and would be slightly later than first departure or earlier than final arrival dates. For central and eastern Nevada, where *Asyndesmus* is almost exclusively transient, all birds are classed simply as migrants.

It is very difficult to untangle records of migrant birds in areas where Lewis woodpeckers are partially resident or show local movement only. Snow (MS) and Woodbury et al. (1949) describe *Asyndesmus* as essentially resident in central Utah, although Behle (1943, 1955, 1958) and Snow (MS) list birds in May and September both inside and outside the normal breeding range apparently in

TABLE 2
TIMING OF SPRING MIGRATION

Locality	Leave winter area average (n); extremes	Arrive breeding area average (n); extremes
British Columbia	no data	3 May (24); 24 April to 16 May
Washington		2 May (18); 22 April to 16 May
Oregon	22 April (1)	24 April (5); 24 March to 15 May
California:		
Breeding in Sierra Nevada and Cascades		11 May (12); 25 April to 29 May
Winter in Central California	19 April (20); 25 March to 3 May	
Winter in Southern California	27 April (14); 2 April to 19 May	
Montana, Idaho and Wyoming		8 May (25); 27 April to 30 May
South Dakota (Black Hills)	no data	last half of May (Pettingill and Whitney, 1965)
Colorado	no data	4 May (7); 23 April to 18 May
Utah (local movement)	First days of April (Snow, MS)	
Nevada:		
Migrants	4 May (7); 23 April to 18 May (?)	
Breeding		from 18 April (N. K. Johnson, MS)
Arizona	28 April (11); 2 April to 18 May	7 May (1); (Woodbury & Russell, 1945)
New Mexico	late March (J. S. Ligon, 1961)	No data

migration. These might be birds moving north from Arizona or south from the northern Rocky Mountains, but their status remains uncertain because of the resident population present. Data on migrants from the Front Range in Colorado and the South Coast Range in California are equivocal due to the presence of resident birds, and also because these areas are both breeding and winter habitats so that a migrant bird might either be leaving or entering the area in both spring and fall. Bailey and Niedrach (1965:491) note in Colorado: "There is a definite seasonal movement, but many winter where food is available, so that it is impossible to determine dates of arrival and departure."

One further problem is that of distinguishing the migrant from the vagrant bird, or the rare individual which may winter in what usually is only breeding habitat (see fig. 1). In tabulating data on migration I have excluded records of birds considered to be vagrant. For example, N. K. Johnson (MS) noted that three Lewis woodpeckers were seen on 29 November, 1954, at 5,000 feet (1,525 meters) in the Virginia Range of western Nevada; *Audubon Field Notes* (1958) reported two birds in Reno, Nevada, during a Christmas count in 1957. I have not included these birds as fall migrants. Several records of uncertain status are designated with question marks in tables 2 and 3.

Despite the problems caused by the complexity and irregularity of Lewis woodpecker movements, tables 2 and 3 do show the general features of *Asyndesmus*

TABLE 3
TIMING OF FALL MIGRATION

Locality	Leave breeding area average (n); extremes	Arrive winter area average (n); extremes
British Columbia.........	23 Sept. (12); 23 August to 26 October	no data
Washington..............	7 Sept. (4); 26 August to 18 Sept. (31 October?) (mid-August to late September, Jewett *et al*, 1953)	
Oregon...................	22 Sept. (4); 21 August to 15 October	
California:		
Breeding in Sierra Nevada and Cascades	21 August (9); 5 August to 20 Sept.	
Winter in Central California............		28 Sept. (22); 28 August to 30 October
Winter in Southern California............		6 October (24); 2 Sept. to 1 November
Montana, Idaho, and Wyoming..............	16 Sept. (21); 16 August to 24 October	
South Dakota (Black Hills).................	last half of August (Pettingill & Whitney, 1965)	no data
Colorado.................	28 Sept. (1)	no data
Utah (local movement)...	late July (Snow, MS)	Sept. (Snow, MS)
Nevada:		
Migrants................	............21 Sept. (11); 2 Sept. to 9 October	
Breeding................		until 11 Sept. (N. K. Johnson, MS)
Arizona..................	7 October (1)	18 October (24); 2 Sept. to 30 November (?)
New Mexico..............	17 Sept. (25); 2 August to 24 October	10 October and 15 October

migration. Most birds arrive on the breeding grounds in early May, and leave between the end of August and the last week in September. Winter populations arrive in late September or the first half of October and usually stay until late April. Lewis woodpeckers arrive on wintering grounds in Arizona later than elsewhere, suggesting a long migration from the north. Likewise, the average date for fall migrants in southern California is later than for the Central Valley (table 3). Pettingill and Whitney (1965) report that Lewis woodpeckers arrive in the

Black Hills, South Dakota, in the last half of May—rather later than in most areas, perhaps due to the remoteness of this breeding range. However, populations in Idaho, Montana, and Wyoming show no similar delay.

FALL NOMADISM

Averaging the arrival and departure dates given in tables 2 and 3 provides an estimate of the duration of spring and fall migration. Lewis woodpeckers left their winter grounds on 22 April (n = 49) and arrived at their breeding grounds on 5 May (n = 95), a "migration" of 13 days. In the fall, birds left nesting areas on 14 September (n = 79) and reached their winter habitat on 7 October (n = 74), a 23 day interval. These data suggesting a more prolonged fall migration are supplemented by a considerable amount of observational evidence that Lewis woodpeckers are nomadic in this season, being especially attracted to sources of native or cultivated fruit before moving on to permanent winter grounds.

Fall nomadism often involves an altitudinal movement. Hand (1941) noted that birds nesting in the St. Joe National Forest in Idaho wandered to higher altitudes after breeding and before migration. In Colorado, Bailey and Niedrach (1965:491) observed that "after the young are on the wing, there is a movement into the mountains, and occasional birds are seen at 10,000 feet or higher." From 22 to 30 July, 1965, a post-breeding flock of adult and juvenile Lewis woodpeckers remained at the head of the Sagehen Creek Basin, 2,200 meters, in Nevada County, California (pl. 3,*a*). The nearest breeding population which I found was at Boca Reservoir, approximately 12 miles to the east and at about 1,800 meters elevation. Breeding birds apparently depart earlier from eastern California than elsewhere (table 3), perhaps moving to the higher mountains to escape the summer drought of that region.

Snow (MS) observed: "Along the Wasatch Mountain Range in north central Utah during the last days of July the flocks of Woodpeckers in the valleys start a movement toward the canyons and mountain valleys. The middle of August finds the valley floors entirely deserted and many flocks high in the mountains. Late September finds a large number of the birds back to the canyon mouths storing acorns."

Asyndesmus which move to higher elevations not only feed upon insects but also take a variety of wild fruits and berries. Gabrielson and Jewett (1940) and Newberry (1857) noted that Lewis woodpeckers compete with robins (*Turdus migratorius*) and bluebirds (*Sialia*) for mountain ash berries (*Fraxinus*) in the fall months. Farner (1952:59) noted that in Crater Lake National Park, Oregon, "flocks of Lewis's Woodpeckers observed in the Park in the fall are invariably feeding on insects, which they catch on the wing, or on berries such as currant, twin-berry, huckleberry, and elderberry." Snow (MS) observed birds feeding upon "choke-cherries and wild berries" during the period of fall nomadism.

Lewis woodpeckers also take wild berries or fruit at low elevations. Nuttall (1840) observed birds feeding on berries along the Willamette River in Oregon, in late August. Between 9 and 16 October, Lamb (1912) recorded about six individuals, in company with flickers (*Colaptes cafer*), taking wild grapes in the Daggett Valley of the Mojave Desert in California.

As a further manifestation of their opportunism, Lewis woodpeckers also wander in fall to orchards where they may take large amounts of cultivated fruit. Ferry (1908) found large flocks present in the orchards of the Beswick Valley in northern California, particularly in the first half of August. The local landowners were killing as many as 50 birds per day in an effort to protect their crops. Walker (1924) observed that they did considerable damage to apple orchards near Blaine, Tillamook County, Oregon. Grinnell and Lamb (1927) noted that Lewis woodpeckers wintering at San José in Baja California took fruit from local pear orchards. Gilman (1936) found *Asyndesmus* feeding upon dates in Death Valley, California, between 11 September and 1 November, 1935.

H. Brown (1902) recorded an invasion of *Asyndesmus* near Tucson, Arizona, between 28 September and 28 October, 1884. On 29 September (op. cit.: 81) "they were mostly feeding on pomegranate fruit," in addition to doing considerable flycatching. By 13 October Brown observed in his field notes (op. cit.: 82): "Now that the pomegranate crop has been destroyed they have commenced to eat the quinces, of which there are large quantities."

Neff (1928) found that Lewis woodpeckers in and around the Rogue River Valley in southern Oregon *both* wandered altitudinally and also invaded local apple orchards during a single fall season. In early July, after breeding, they began to move up out of the valley into the Cascade Range to the east. By late July scarcely any remained. In August they were common in the mountains at Klamath and around Crater Lake. In September tremendous numbers moved back into the valley and began taking apples, doing considerable damage to some orchards before settling in oak woodland to winter.

Opportunism

Nesting season.—Breeding *Asyndesmus* concentrate in areas where free-living insects are abundant. Their opportunism often is striking in this regard. One unusual example is the observation of Kitchin (1949) who discovered Lewis woodpeckers feeding upon insects associated with drift-wood and logs washed up on the beach at Kalaloch, on the Olympic Peninsula of Washington. When certain insects such as grasshoppers and locusts reach plague proportions, Lewis woodpeckers are known to respond accordingly. In July, 1904, J. J. Williams (1905) discovered a breeding population in the Sardine Valley, Nevada County, California, associated with a tremendous outbreak of grasshoppers which had begun the previous year; he noted that there seemed to be a nest in almost every dead pine or stump in and around the valley. Sheldon (1907) likewise found Lewis woodpeckers nesting in areas where grasshoppers were numerous near Eagle Lake, California. Munro (1930) recorded a huge increase in numbers of this woodpecker during the breeding seasons of 1927 and 1928, correlated with swarms of grasshoppers and crickets in the Okanagan Valley of British Columbia.

From 1965 to 1968 I observed a number of Lewis woodpeckers nesting near Boca Reservoir which fed extensively on the larvae of the Great Basin tent caterpillar (*Malacosoma fragile* Stretch). Clark (1956) states that this lepidopteran is subject to periodic outbreaks on bitter-brush (*Purshia tridentata*) in widespread parts of eastern California, and that the Truckee basin stands (near Boca

Reservoir) have supported small colonies of *M. fragile* since 1950. The *Asyndesmus* I studied fed almost exclusively on these caterpillars, especially feeding them to their young. The birds reared young from late June through the first week in August, when *M. fragile* were present in an advanced instar stage. Clark (op. cit.) found that the eggs hatched from mid-May to early June, and pupation occurred from mid-July to mid-August in the Truckee area. According to Clark, the caterpillar occasionally reaches densities at which the *Purshia* plants may be defoliated and killed. Although there appear to be no records of breeding Lewis woodpeckers concentrating upon these plagues, the behavior of the small population near Boca suggests that these birds might respond in a manner similar to that observed during locust swarms.

Lewis woodpeckers are capable of nesting semi-gregariously, which would facilitate breeding in areas of abundant food should nest sites be scarce. Along the Columbia River in Oregon, Currier (1928) discovered two cottonwood trees about 400 meters apart, each of which contained three active Lewis woodpeckers nests. Snow (MS) found two nests in one tree, with another in a second tree 3 meters distant, near Centerville, Utah. Although I have never observed more than one nest per tree, birds breeding in the San Antonio Valley and at Boca Reservoir nested within 15 meters of each other without any noticeable strife.

Because *Asyndesmus* respond to fluctuations in insect populations their presence in a particular breeding area varies from year to year. This periodicity also may be the result of certain habitats being only temporarily suitable. This is especially the case in logged or burned forests, which are good Lewis woodpecker habitat for only a limited time prior to regeneration of second growth timber (see "Habitat and Distribution"). Dawson and Bowles (1909:51) make the significant comment that Lewis woodpeckers breed *regularly* in open pine and cottonwood in eastern Washington, while "their occurrence west of the Cascades is subject to little understood fluctuations." They noted that *Asyndesmus* breeds largely in burned areas in the west, and the short-term nature of this habitat would very probably account for the observed irregularity in abundance.

Winter.—Although no regular data are available on yearly acorn yields, most observers agree that Lewis woodpeckers concentrate in winter where the acorn crop is high. F. M. Bailey (1928) noted that in New Mexico they usually wintered near abundant acorn supplies. Neff (1928) found *Asyndesmus* common in the oaks of the Rogue River Valley of Oregon in the winter of 1924–25, but none was present during the 1925–26 season, which was a very poor one for acorns in that valley. Regarding Colorado populations, Bailey and Niedrach (1965:491) state: "Apparently there is a considerable change in populations through the years for in the early 1920's Lewis' Woodpeckers were very common in the Daniels Park area, and then for a period of twenty-five years, the species was almost absent from that region. During the winter and summer of 1957–58, the woodpeckers again were numerous and they were the most conspicuous birds of the pine and oak country, possibly due to the heavy acorn crop."

Welch (1899:29) observed "hundreds" of birds near Copperopolis, Calaveras County, California, in the fall of 1898, and noted that mast also was plentiful that year. *Audubon Field Notes* (1952) observers noticed that a lack of Lewis woodpeckers in southern California in the fall of 1951 was coincident with low acorn production. *Audubon Field Notes* (1957) reported that Lewis woodpeckers invaded the Paynes Creek area in Tehama County, California, in the fall of 1956, when again the acorn crop was particularly good.

The band-tailed pigeon (*Columba fasciata*) is another species which feeds opportunistically upon acorns in the winter (Neff, 1947). It is of interest that influxes of these birds and Lewis woodpeckers occasionally occur together. *Audubon Field Notes* (1951) reported that *Asyndesmus* reappeared after a two year absence at Granite Station in southern California in October of 1950, where they, along with flocks of band-tailed pigeons, harvested the large acorn crop of that fall. In the winter of 1965–66 I found both species common on Mt. Hamilton, Santa Clara County, California, but neither wintered there the following year when acorn crops were low. Several *Audubon Field Notes* Christmas counts in California show similar correlations between Lewis woodpeckers and band-tailed pigeons. At Redlands, 221 pigeons and 6 *Asyndesmus* were counted in 1954. No woodpeckers and 10 or fewer pigeons were found there in the two years preceding and following. In the Pauma Valley, 5 Lewis woodpeckers and 194 pigeons were reported in 1948, with only 2 *Asyndesmus* and 15 pigeons being counted in the next three years combined. At Big Bear Lake, 63 *Asyndesmus* and 300 band-tailed pigeons were counted in 1941, while neither species was recorded in 1940 or from 1942 to 1951.

Almond and other commercial mast sources are more extensive and regular than acorn production, so that *Asyndesmus* populations are more predictable in orchard areas. Nevertheless, the fact that these woodpeckers have come to utilize this particularly rich food source, as well as soft cultivated fruits in the fall, is further evidence of their general opportunism. Certainly those populations in central California which I have discovered using green almonds in the spring to feed their young show marked behavioral and ecological plasticity.

FEEDING ECOLOGY AND BEHAVIOR

INTRODUCTION

Asyndesmus lewis is one of the most aerial of woodpeckers, and early naturalists in western North America were uniformly impressed with its flycatching behavior. Baird, Brewer, and Ridgway (1875:564) describe "a very peculiar and characteristic habit of ascending high into the air, and taking a strange, floating flight, seemingly laborious as if struggling against the wind, and then descending in broad circles to the trees." This is a good description of the prolonged hawking flights which Lewis woodpeckers execute. Cooper (1870:407) observed that "they keep much about the higher parts of the trees, circling around them in pursuit of insects, and not troubling themselves much to hammer the bark for food." Beal (1911:46), on the basis of stomach content analyses, found that the diet was about 37 percent animal and 63 percent vegetable and concluded that "there is nothing in the stomachs to indicate that this bird ever digs into wood, decayed or otherwise, in search of beetle larvae."

It seems that Lewis woodpeckers feed largely upon adult emergent insects, complemented by fruits and mast during fall and winter months when such insects are less plentiful. This section describes feeding behavior in both a qualitative and quantitative manner, with regard to the various foraging techniques employed and the seasonal changes therein. First a brief discussion of structural adaptations for feeding is relevant, especially in comparison with other species of woodpeckers.

STRUCTURAL ADAPTATIONS

It is possible to recognize three broad ecological types among North American woodpeckers, each centering around a type of food niche. Not all species fit neatly into one or the other category, nor are the categories necessarily intended to imply

TABLE 4
WING DIMENSIONS OF WOODPECKERS

Species	Wt. (gms)	Wing area $(cm)^2$	Wing length (cm)	Wing span (cm)	Aspect ratio	Load (gm/cm^2)
Dendrocopos major........	73.0	238	12.95	42.2	7.48	0.31
Melanerpes formicivorus..	74.5	306	14.11	44.0†	6.33	0.24
Centurus carolinus.....	87.0	262	13.10	41.0†	6.41	0.33
Colaptes auratus.......	100.0	324	15.63	44.0†	5.97	0.31
Asyndesmus lewis.........	106.0	535	17.36*	53.0	5.25	0.20

* Data are from study skins in the Museum of Vertebrate Zoology, University of California, Berkeley.
† Estimated from preserved specimens in the Museum of Vertebrate Zoology.

phylogenetic relationships, but the groupings are valuable for comparing structural modifications.

The first group could be termed the "ground type," and is represented in North America by the flickers (*Colaptes*). These birds forage extensively on the ground, particularly for ants, and are the least arboreal members of the family (Beal, 1911; Bent, 1939). Second is a group of "classical" woodpeckers, consisting of species which obtain their food largely by chiseling and scaling living or dead wood to extract insect larvae. Members of the genus *Dendrocopos*, the three-toed woodpeckers (*Picoides*), and the pileated (*Dryocopus pileatus*) and ivory-billed (*Campephilus principalis*) woodpeckers best fit this category. Finally there are relatively omnivorous species which rely to a greater or lesser degree upon emergent insects when available, shifting to fruits, nuts, and berries at other times. Boring for larvae occurs infrequently if at all, and is replaced by gleaning and flycatching for adult insects. Because these birds are more dependent upon seasonal food sources, they often store or cache nuts for use during the winter months. Most typical of the last group are the red-headed (*Melanerpes erythrocephalus*), acorn (*M. formicivorus*), and Lewis woodpeckers.

Wing dimensions.—Table 4 gives wing data for various species in the family Picidae. The measurements for *Asyndesmus* are those of Baldwin and Schneider (1963); the remainder are from various sources compiled by Greenwalt (1962), except as noted. Wing length is defined as the distance from the tip to the first joint, while wing span is the distance from tip to tip when the wings are spread. Aspect ratio is the ratio of wing span to wing width, or chord (Savile, 1957).

Weight-specific wing dimensions decrease with increasing body size (Greenwalt, op. cit.). However, *Asyndesmus* and *Melanerpes formicivorus*, two flycatching species, both have disproportionately large wing areas and thus small wing loads (table 4) in comparison with the similar sized *Colaptes*, a terrestrial species, and *Dendrocopos major*, an Old World species which feeds upon woodboring larvae (Witherby et al., 1943). The Lewis woodpecker has a lighter wing load than *Melanerpes formicivorus* and is the stronger flycatcher of the two. Burt (1930) found that the humerus and ulna are longer in *Asyndesmus, Melanerpes formicivorus, M. erythrocephalus*, and *Centurus carolinus* than in *Dendrocopos villosus* and *Picoides*.

It is significant that while wing areas are greater, the aspect ratios of the Lewis and acorn woodpeckers are relatively small (table 4). In other words, these two species have broader rather than longer wings. Savile (1957) points out that narrow wings are suited for high speed flight, as seen in swallows, swifts, and falcons, while broad wings increase maneuverability and lift at low velocities. Lewis woodpeckers often circle slowly while on hawking flights, and execute sharp turns when actually capturing flying insects. For this broad wings would be highly advantageous.

Skull structure.—All woodpeckers have skulls specially constructed to withstand hard blows, since all at least use the bill to excavate nest holes. The nasofrontal hinge and interorbital septum, where most blow impact is absorbed, are relatively sturdy. *Mm. protractor pterygoidei*, which originates on the interorbital septum and inserts on the orbital process of the pterygoid bone, is large in woodpeckers and acts to brace the upper mandible against hammering blows (see Spring, 1965, and W. Bock, 1966, for a discussion of this phenomenon).

It is not surprising that woodpeckers which use the bill for food-getting as well as for nest construction show these skull adaptations best. Burt (1930) pointed out that *Picoides* and *Dendrocopos* have relatively broader skulls than *Asyndesmus* and other flycatching-frugivorous types. He also noticed that the frontal bones fold anteriorly out over the nasals in those species which do the most digging; this folding presumably reinforces the naso-frontal hinge and reduces cranial kinesis. Spring (1965) found that *Asyndesmus* had the greatest gape of a number of species examined, and observed that this would facilitate flycatching.

Mm. protractor pterygoidei and the orbital process of the pterygoid are relatively larger in *Dendrocopos villosus* and *Picoides arcticus* than in less arboreal species (table 5). I examined a single preserved specimen of each of the species listed in the table, and measured the maximum width of the muscles on a line parallel to the upper mandible. Orbital processes were measured from dried skulls. Measurements are compared with the length of four thoracic vertebrae, after Spring (1965). *Asyndesmus* clearly shows the poorest development of this muscle system, while *Melanerpes formicivorus* shows a great amount of development for a flycatching-frugivorous type (table 5). This difference may be related to different techniques of acorn storage. While *Asyndesmus* and *Melanerpes erythrocephalus* store mast in natural cracks and crevices (Kilham, 1958a; personal observation), *M. formicivorus* usually digs holes for each nut stored, and therefore does more hammering than the other species.

Limb and tail characteristics.—Bock and Miller (1959) argue that the zygodactyl foot, with toes one (hallux) and four directed posteriorly and two and three

TABLE 5
Size of Mm. *protractor pterygoidei* and the Orbital Process of Woodpeckers

Species	Muscle width	Muscle*	Orbital process length	n	Process*
Red-shafted flicker (*Colaptes cafer*)	4.2 mm	24%	1.85 mm	10	11.0%
Red-headed woodpecker (*Melanerpes erythrocephalus*)	3.9 mm	26%	0.80 mm	4	5.4%
Lewis woodpecker (*Asyndesmus lewis*)	3.5 mm	20%	0.61 mm	5	3.5%
Acorn woodpecker (*Melanerpes formicivorus*)	4.3 mm	29%	1.30 mm	10	8.6%
Sapsucker (*Sphyrapicus varius*)	3.0 mm	24%	1.27 mm	10	10.2%
Hairy woodpecker (*Dendrocopos villosus*)	4.7 mm	32%	2.82 mm	10	19.0%
Three-toed woodpecker (*Picoides arcticus*)	4.9 mm	33%	2.64 mm	4	17.8%

* Calculated as percentage of four thoracic vertebrae.

anteriorly, is an adaptation for perching on the ground or on horizontal rather than vertical surfaces. Most woodpeckers (including *Asyndesmus*) direct the fourth toes laterally when resting or climbing on a vertical surface, resulting in an efficient pincer-like grip with both feet. The fourth toes are moved posteriorly into a true zygodactyl position only when this bird is on a horizontal limb. Only the flickers, least arboreal of North American species, possess permanently zygodactyl feet, which Bock and Miller consider to be a primitive character shared with *Jynx* and *Picumnus*. Flickers also have relatively longer legs than other woodpeckers (Spring, 1965), perhaps related to their terrestrial feeding habits. Lewis woodpeckers have the shortest legs, followed by other flycatching-frugivorous types, while the arboreal species are intermediate (Spring, op. cit.). *Asyndesmus* shows an interesting parallel to the true flycatchers (Tyrannidae) in having such small limbs.

Burt (1929, 1930) found that *Picoides* and *Dendrocopos* have larger pygostyle discs for the insertion of tail muscles, and that the shafts of the central rectrices also are more specialized for support in these species. He (1929, fig. 5) pictures the central rectrices as most strongly reinforced in *Dendrocopos*, least so in *Colaptes*, with *Melanerpes formicivorus* intermediate. I found *Asyndesmus* comparable to the latter in rectrix development.

In summary, the Lewis woodpecker has broader wings with a lighter load, smaller legs, and a skull less specialized to absorb hard blows and capable of

TABLE 6
SEXUAL DIMORPHISM IN SIZE IN *Asyndesmus lewis**

Item	Sex	n	Mean and range (mm)	Standard error	Standard deviation	Coefficient of variation	Coefficient of difference	Percent dimorphism
Wing length	♂	47	168.2 (159.1–175.2)	0.60	4.11	2.44	0.694	3.97%
	♀	31	161.8 (153.3–168.1)	0.92	5.15	3.18		
Tail length	♂	39	100.4 (94.3–106.2)	0.55	3.44	3.31	0.440	3.21%
	♀	30	97.3 (89.8–103.2)	0.67	3.67	3.77		
Bill length	♂	51	24.4 (22.4–27.8)	0.22	1.54	6.31	0.702	9.36%
	♀	38	22.3 (20.1–24.7)	0.24	1.45	6.50		
Tarsus length	♂	52	25.6 (23.5–27.9)	0.13	0.95	3.71	0.574	4.57%
	♀	38	24.5 (21.8–26.5)	0.16	1.00	4.08		

* Based upon specimens from the Museum of Vertebrate Zoology, University of California, Berkeley, collected mainly from the Pacific coast region.

greater gape, than other members of the family Picidae in North America. These structural characteristics are correlated with the species' feeding behavior.

SEXUAL DIMORPHISM

Male Lewis woodpeckers are larger than females, more so in bill length than in wing, tail, or tarsus length (table 6). Davis (1965) and Selander and Giller (1963) have shown that sexual dimorphism in bill length exceeds that in other size characters in most species of woodpeckers. Selander (1966) discusses the role of bill dimorphism in reducing intraspecific competition and presents evidence that in *Centurus striatus* of Hispaniola, in which the bill of the female averaged 21.3 percent shorter than that of the male, there is a demonstrable difference in feeding behavior between the sexes. Males use the longer bill to do more probing, while the short-billed females do more surface gleaning. In the continental *C. aurifrons*, in which bill dimorphism is only about 9 percent, differences in foraging behavior are not as marked. Selander argues that the exaggerated dimorphism of *C. striatus* results in an expanded food niche and thus a lessening of intraspecific competition, and that this is possible because of the lack of interspecific competition in the case of this island endemic. Kilham (1965) and J. D. Ligon (1968) have demonstrated niche dimorphism in *Dendrocopos villosus, D. borealis, D. stricklandi,* and *D. arizonae*.

Davis (1965:566) suggests that "bill size would probably be the most important character involved" in determining the range in size of food items taken and the foraging techniques employed by a bird. Bill dimorphism and variation in bill length, which Davis found generally high in *Dendrocopos* species, could be directly related to niche expansion. It is not altogether clear how this might apply to *Asyndesmus*, although dimorphism and variation are high (table 6) for bill length. During the breeding season flycatching and ground-brush foraging predominate (table 7). These foraging methods are not tied to bill length in as obvious a way as are the excavation techniques used by more "typical" woodpeckers (e.g., *Centurus, Dendrocopos*). Moreover, the one time when the bill of *Asyndesmus* is most essential is when the birds are shelling and storing acorns; and, of course, this is the same process for both sexes.

Although males could be taking larger food items than females I have been unable to detect any qualitative or quantitative differences in foraging techniques employed. Lewis woodpeckers are opportunistic during the breeding season, concentrating on temporarily abundant prey populations. Field observations show that both sexes respond to changes in insect populations by switching to whichever prey species is particularly abundant at any given time (see p. 39). Root (1967) observed similar opportunistic feeding behavior in the blue-gray gnatcatcher (*Polioptila caerulea*). Niche dimorphism is unlikely in these instances on theoretical grounds, since selection should favor the ability of both sexes to exploit the full range of food types. That is, if most important prey species become abundant sequentially, each sex should be unspecialized enough to feed upon all types. If selection is to favor a partitioning of the food niche, it is necessary that different prey items be equally available simultaneously.

It is important to realize that the selection pressures of intraspecific competition can act only to increase in already established sexual dimorphism. In a theoretical monomorphic population, a large female would have the same advantages as a large male in exploiting foods unavailable to the bulk of the population. While individual variability might increase there would be no reason to expect sexual dimorphism to occur. The question then arises as to what degree of dimorphism has resulted from sexual selection and what degree from ecological

TABLE 7
FEEDING BEHAVIOR

I. Breeding habitat—pine forest (305.9 min.)		
Flycatching:	177.0 min.	(57.9%)
Ground-brush:	98.1 min.	(32.1%)
Gleaning:	30.8 min.	(10.0%)
II. Winter habitat—orchard and oak woodland (1371.9 min.)		
Acorn and nut stores:	982.6 min.	(71.5%)
Flycatching:	207.9 min.	(15.2%)
Gleaning:	181.4 min.	(13.3%)
III. Breeding habitat—oak woodland (214.3 min.)		
Flycatching:	97.4 min.	(45.5%)
Gleaning:	37.5 min.	(17.5%)
Ground-brush:	55.6 min.	(25.9%)
Acorn stores:	23.8 min.	(11.1%)

selection. It seems certain that in such highly dimorphic forms as *Centurus striatus* and the New Zealand huia (*Neomorpha acutirostris*) ecological selection has played a role. The absence of interspecific competition may have played a role in the marked niche expansion of these insular species. Selander (1966:128) points out that a species might exhibit niche dimorphism secondarily as a result of size differences established through sexual selection alone. Such a hypothesis is easier to demonstrate for a given species than it is to negate, but at present I feel there is no basis for ascribing a sexual niche dimorphism to *Asyndesmus*.

FEEDING BEHAVIOR

Flycatching.—Lewis woodpeckers initiate hawking flights from prominent scanning perches. These perches vary from low stumps or fence posts to the tops of the tallest trees, depending upon what sorts of insects the birds are hunting. Hawking perches usually are isolated and conspicuous, affording a clear view of the surrounding area (pl. 1,*b*). Dead trees, power poles, and fenceposts comprised 72 percent of 662 perches from which I observed birds making hawking flights. The remainder were in living trees. Individuals seem to have specific preferred hawking perches. In 534 of 716 observed flights, the bird returned and began scanning again from the point of origin.

Scanning is an important element of flycatching behavior. Birds perch either horizontally or on vertical surfaces, and search the area where insects are flying. The head is not moved continuously, but is passed through a series of fixed positions, each of which is held for one or two seconds, until a flying insect is located. The head is rotated in order to scan on a horizontal plane, and is cocked to one side or the other to cover areas both above and below the perch. Although the actual approach to the prey item is head-on and may permit binocular evaluation, scanning is largely a monocular phenomenon. Once an insect is located, a bird often will move its head quickly from one position to another just prior to taking flight. I interpret this as triangulation—an attempt to estimate the distance to the flying insect.

Scanning time between hawking flights varies considerably. In winter, birds usually scanned while simultaneously working over their storage sites. Thus it was not possible to determine exactly how long a bird spent in locating a prey item,

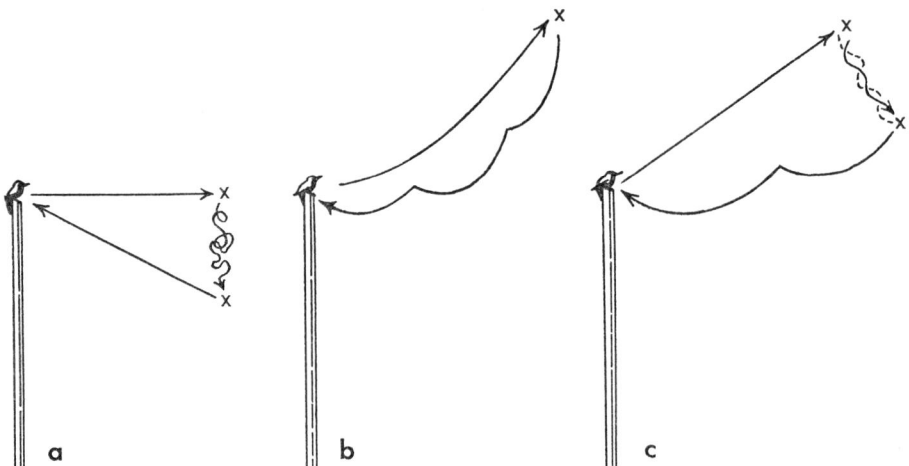

Fig. 2. Patterns of hawking flights by Lewis woodpeckers: (a) bird flies to insect on level with perch; insect drops to avoid capture; (b) bird flies to insect above perch, returning in series of descending arches (see text); (c) insect higher than perch drops to avoid capture; bird executes one stall on return flight.

versus the time spent flying to and capturing it. During the breeding season, however, individuals often fed exclusively by flycatching for long periods, and appeared to search continuously during the intervals between flights. Birds nesting at Boca Reservoir, in open and burned pine forest, scanned for an average of 31 seconds between hawking flights; scanning comprised about two-thirds of the total time spent flycatching. In the oak woodland of the San Antonio Valley scanning intervals averaged 22 seconds and comprised 53 percent of recorded flycatching time (table 7).

Lewis woodpeckers have remarkable eyesight. I have seen them fly from hawking perches as far as 60 meters to capture specific flying insects, although most flights are much shorter. Movement to the prey is direct, with steady, crow-like wingbeats. However, an insect usually flies or drops erratically in an effort to escape predation. The woodpecker must execute elaborate maneuvers to make the final capture. It is not unusual to see a bird fly steadily toward an insect, and then suddenly tumble toward the ground. The bird actually is falling with the insect while simultaneously trying to capture it (fig. 2). The method is clumsy in appearance, but it usually is successful. The return to the hawking perch is by direct flight if the capture was made below or level with the perch. If the insect is taken high above the perch, the bird either circles down or descends in a long glide broken by somewhat regular stalls. The wings are pulled in, causing a rapid drop, and then extended, causing the bird to "pull up" briefly. The entire return resembles a series of descending arches (fig. 2).

Not all hawking flights are specific; I apply the term to a hawking flight that is directed at one particular prey item. When this insect is taken the bird returns to its hawking perch. Lewis woodpeckers at times remain in the air for several minutes or more, foraging like a swallow or swift, and taking more than one insect per flight. Scanning is largely eliminated in these non-specific flights, when the density of flying insects is high, and the probability of chance encounters is great. Twelve percent of 677 flights I observed could be classed as non-specific. Rathbun (in Bent, 1939) observed a pair of Lewis woodpeckers flying back and forth over a meadow along with barn and cliff swallows. He observed these birds for more than half an hour, and both were continuously in flight during that time. The longest flight which I have observed lasted 8 minutes.

The average time for a sample of 677 flights was 16.5 seconds, with a range of 2 to 480 seconds, and a median of 8 seconds. Figure 3 shows the frequency distribution of this sample, divided into one winter and two breeding habitat categories. There was a marked variation in hawking flight times. This variation was most extreme for birds breeding in the oak woodland of the San Antonio Valley. Here nearly half of the flights were short sallies of 5 seconds or less, made out between the oaks. In addition, however, there were a number of very long, non-specific flights made high over the oaks. In all three habitats the great majority of hawking flights were less than 20 seconds in duration (fig. 3) and were of the specific type.

One final point to be made about flycatching is that it is not usually a random feeding behavior. That is, although a great variety of hawking flights occurs (varying in height, duration, number of prey items captured, etc.), nothing approaching the complete repertoire is seen on a daily or hourly basis. Rather, Lewis woodpeckers tend to concentrate on one or a few insect species which are particularly abundant at a given time, and modify their foraging behavior accordingly. Two examples show this well.

On the east side of Boca Reservoir, at Mills Spring, there is a wet meadow which is covered with water in early spring and which dries gradually during the summer. On 8 June, 1966, a large flight of unidentified dipterans was emerging from the rapidly disappearing waters of this meadow. Four Lewis woodpeckers from two nearby nests were feeding almost exclusively by making long flights through the swarms of emerging flies. The average flight lasted 40 seconds (n = 24), well above the overall average in figure 3. These hawking flights were non-specific, in that a number of the small dipterans were taken during each one. Most of the foraging was done between 1 and 10 meters over the meadow where the concentration of flies was the greatest.

Between Boca Reservoir and Mills Spring is a hill covered with greenleaf manzanita (*Arctostaphylos patula*), golden currant (*Ribes aureum*), and tobacco

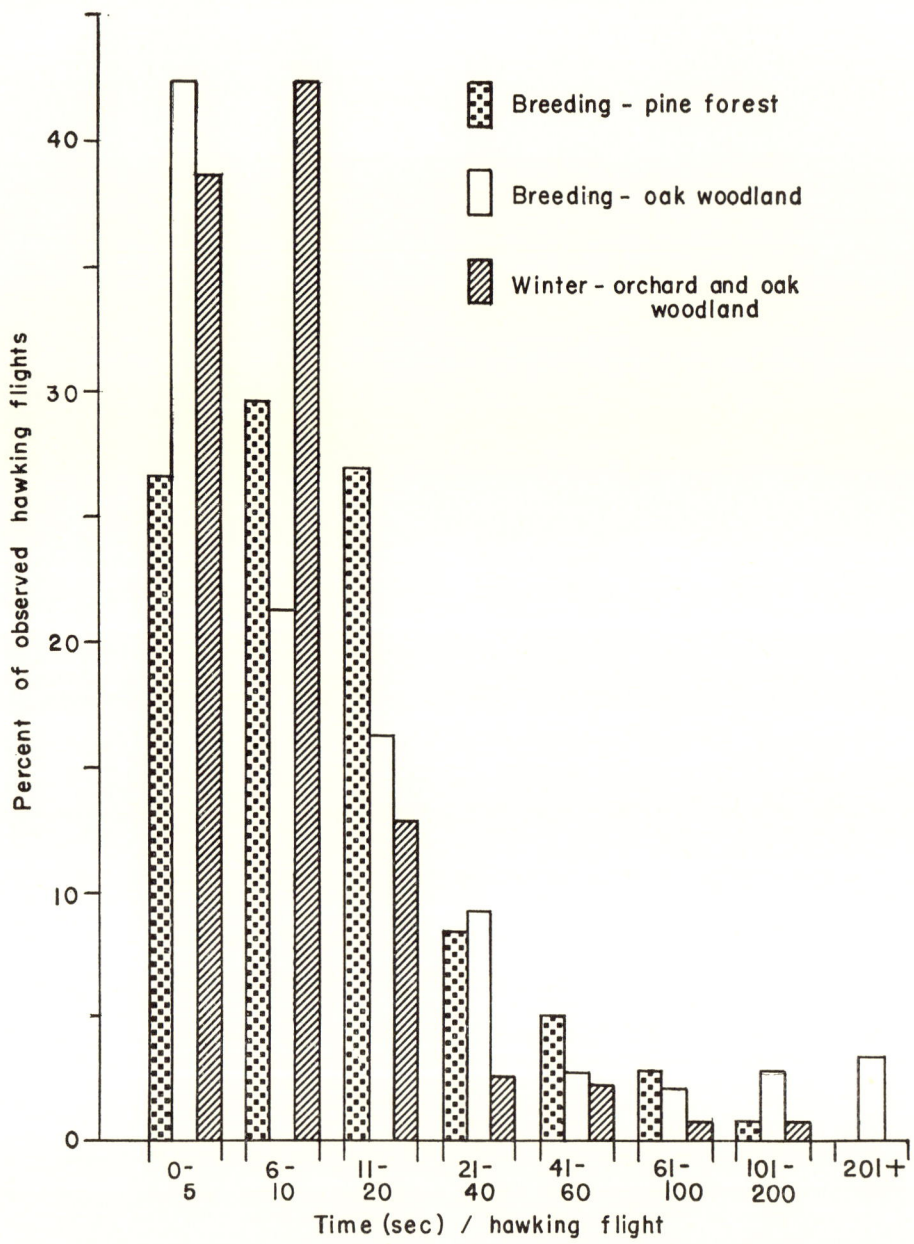

Fig. 3. Duration of hawking flights by Lewis woodpeckers in different habitats.

brush (*Ceanothus velutinus*). Beneath this dense brush lie the decayed logs of an old burn. On the morning of 19 July, 1966, a flight of winged carpenter ants (*Campanotus* sp.) was emerging from these logs. Lewis woodpeckers from surrounding nests concentrated in the area and fed intensively upon the ants. For hawking perches they used the scattered burned stubs which were still standing among the brush. Flights averaged 10 seconds (n = 86) and were specific. A bird scanned until it located a flying ant, flew out and captured it, and returned to a hawking perch.

Ground-brush foraging.—Lewis woodpeckers forage extensively during the breeding season directly on the ground or in low brush (table 7). This behavior, like flycatching, usually is specific; it involves scanning from low stumps, bushes, or the sides of tree trunks, for insects moving over the substrate. Ground-brush foraging appears to be oriented solely toward visible prey. I have never seen a bird dig for soil or litter insects. Scanning is important. It comprised 54 percent of the recorded ground-brush foraging time (table 7). The average scanning interval was 35 seconds (n = 140).

Ground and brush foraging is more restricted to the vicinity of the perch than flycatching; terrestrial insects apparently are not detectable at such great distances. Usually birds captured prey within 3 meters of their hawking perches. In the oak woodland of the San Antonio Valley, Lewis woodpeckers often preyed upon insects moving in the grass understory. When scanning they perched vertically on the sides of oak trunks within 1.5 meters of the ground. Nearly all captures were made close to these hawking positions because it was not possible to see down into the grass except from directly above. At Boca Reservoir, Lewis woodpeckers preyed upon large beetles (*Tenebrio* sp.), which were taken as they crawled over the ground in openings in the brush. The birds used old burned stumps or the brush itself for scanning, but they covered only one or two clearings from any given perch.

Ground-brush foraging maneuvers averaged 30 seconds longer than aerial flights (fig. 4). This is because a larger proportion were of a non-specific nature. Thirty-two percent of the ground-brush feeding periods were non-specific, as compared with 12 percent of the aerial flights. Figure 4 shows the frequency distribution of ground-brush foraging maneuvers observed in the Boca Reservoir and San Antonio Valley areas. As with hawking flights, average length exceeded median length due to occasional very long foraging bouts. The birds in the San Antonio Valley executed many non-specific bouts; most were between 50 and 100 seconds long (fig. 4). These involved predation upon small grassland insects, particularly the larvae of ladybird beetles (*Coccinellidae*). The birds dropped into the grass and took several larvae before returning to feed their young. Even in these cases, however, foraging was not entirely random. A bird would scan motionless for one or two seconds, move to a larva and seize it, and then repeat the process. In this way a bird often moved up to 1 or 1.5 meters through the grass during a single foraging maneuver.

At Boca Reservoir a very important prey species was the Great Basin tent caterpillar (*Malacosoma fragile*). Although Root (1966) found the oak-dwelling *M. constrictum* generally to be distasteful to birds, presumably because of the fine hairs covering their bodies, *Asyndesmus* foraged extensively on the equally hairy *M. fragile* and fed them to their young during fledging. The phytophagous *M. fragile* larvae were abundant on bitter-brush (*Purshia tridentata*) from 1965 through 1968. Lewis woodpeckers took them by scanning from burned stumps, then flying onto the bushes and taking one or two larvae. These maneuvers usually were short and specific, although occasionally a bird searched about in the brush

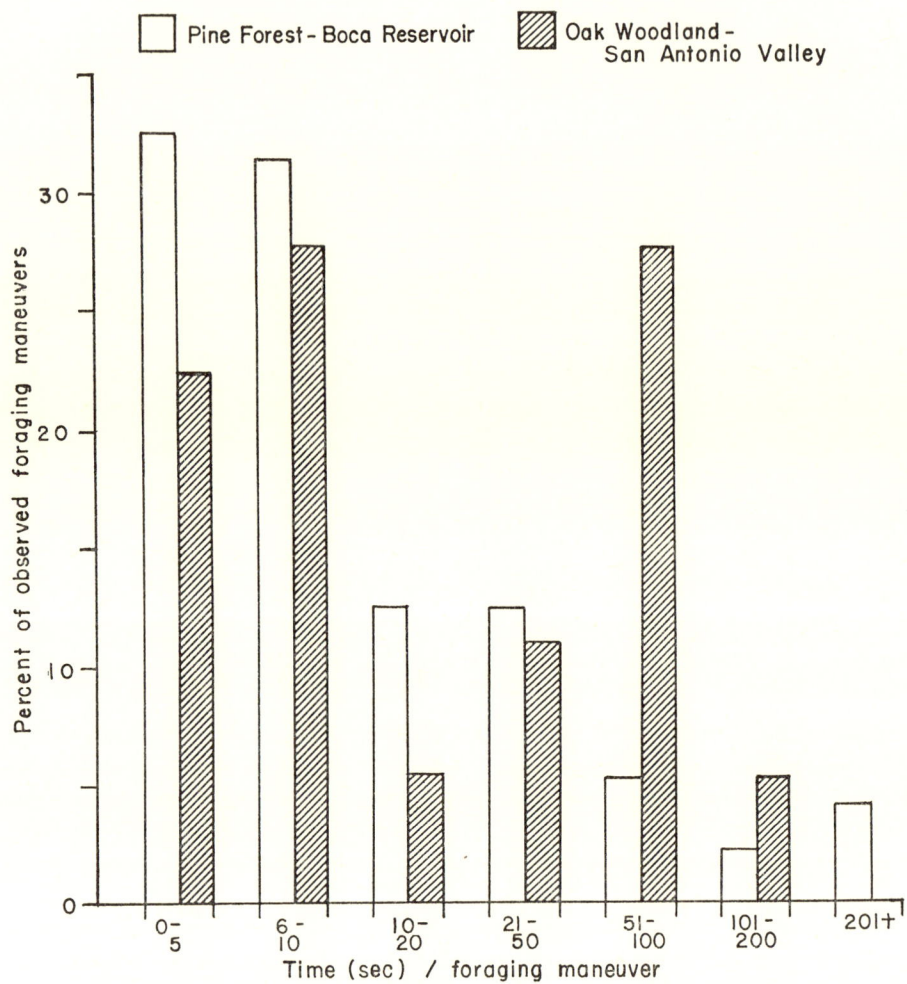

Fig. 4. Duration of ground-brush foraging maneuvers by Lewis woodpeckers in two breeding habitats.

for as long as four minutes (fig. 4), taking a large number of the caterpillars.

Asyndesmus showed considerable agility in moving over the outer branches of the *Purshia* plants. Birds often balanced between two limbs, with legs spread apart, holding one branch with each foot, and reaching out for larvae that were feeding on the fresh foliage of the branch tips. The tail was used as a prop only sporadically during this behavior. At other times individuals perched crosswise on small vertical branches, one foot above the other, with the body parallel to the ground. Occasionally I saw birds hanging from below small horizontal branches, with their bodies perpendicular to the branch axes, and with tails pulled ventrally in the manner of foraging chickadees.

These foraging patterns are remarkable for a woodpecker, as are the prolonged aerial flights. However, such behavioral plasticity might be expected in as highly an opportunistic species as *Asyndesmus*. While most woodpeckers are relatively specialized foragers, selection seems to have favored the ability of Lewis woodpeckers to respond to high densities of almost all kinds of free-living insects.

Gleaning.—Lewis woodpeckers prey upon insects living on the limbs and trunks of trees by probing into natural crevices, chipping or flaking off small pieces of bark, and most often simply by searching over the limb surfaces. Foraging in trees is restricted to this type of gleaning; I have never observed a bird actually excavating for sub-surface insects. Beal (1911) likewise found no evidence from stomach content analyses to suggest that *Asyndesmus* ever chisels into trees for wood-boring prey.

In their gleaning behavior, Lewis woodpeckers show the most similarity to other members of the family Picidae. However, gleaning occurs less than flycatching and ground-brush foraging in summer, and is secondary to acorn storage in winter (table 7). The birds breeding in the Boca area did very little gleaning; but in oak woodland gleaning was seen both in summer and winter.

Gleaning birds move vertically and peripherally, beginning at the bases of limbs and progressing out toward smaller branches. On the larger limbs, movement is in the typical woodpecker fashion, hitching along with the tail used as a prop and the laterally directed fourth toes acting in juxtaposition as a pincer (see Bock and Miller, 1959). Birds usually maintain this stance while gleaning on horizontal as well as vertical surfaces, and when moving over the undersides of larger branches. Gleaning birds also forage on the finer twigs and outer branches where the usual stance is not possible. Here I observed maneuvering similar to that shown by birds foraging in *Purshia* for tent caterpillars.

A gleaning Lewis woodpecker progresses slowly, two or three hitches at a time, alternated with periods of probing, light tapping, or simple visual searching. Occasionaly a bird will pound vigorously in one spot, and then perch motionless for several seconds. Examination never revealed any evidence of excavation at these sites. Davis (1965:542) observed that foraging *Dendrocopos stricklandi* in Arizona often tapped lightly, waited for a few seconds, and then either began to excavate or moved to a new area. The light tapping presumably would induce wood-boring insects present to move, and thus be detected. Such behavior in *Asyndesmus* could be an attempt to flush insects from crevices or from under bark, but I was never able to record an actual capture following such a burst of hammering.

Gleaning is not as specific as flycatching or ground-brush foraging since no real scanning period is involved. Nevertheless, it often is oriented visually. On 22 June, 1967, in the San Antonio Valley 2,250 of 2,745 bird-seconds of recorded foraging time involved birds gleaning over the limbs and trunks of oak trees. Examination showed that this unusual amount of gleaning was directed toward large numbers of ants moving in the trees on that date. The ants were so numerous that an average gleaning period lasted only 38.6 seconds (n = 58) before the bird returned to feed its young. This foraging clearly was visual, since the birds fed without probing or tapping, but simply by picking ants off the bark.

The particular specialization of Lewis woodpeckers as predators seems to be their emphasis upon visual stimuli, since most of their prey is free-living. Insect movement is critical in flycatching, ground-brush foraging, and often in gleaning.

In contrast, woodpeckers which feed upon wood-boring insects (e.g., *Picoides, Dryocopus, Dendrocopos*) must locate prey from the sounds which these insects make (Davis, 1965:542–3; Ramp, 1965), or through some knowledge of where they are likely to occur.

Acorn and almond stores.—Lewis woodpeckers store acorns in the fall for use as food during the winter (table 7). Commercial nut crops, particularly almonds, often are used instead of acorns, but the behavior related to storage and utilization remains essentially the same. Each individual bird (or rarely a pair) harvests, stores, and maintains its own cache of nuts, which it defends throughout the winter against other birds (see "Competition"). Most of the data presented in this section were taken from birds wintering near Livermore, Alameda County, California. Almonds from local groves were the major source of mast, along with a few walnuts and acorns. The birds used old power poles with desiccation cracks as storage sites, and roosted in oaks or sycamores in the area. I also studied birds wintering in the almond groves of the Capay Valley, Solano County, in the oak woodland of Mt. Hamilton and the San Antonio Valley, Santa Clara County, and in the riparian oak woodland along the Old River near Tracy, San Joaquin County, California.

The storing process can be divided into three stages: harvesting the nut, shelling it, and storing the mast. A Lewis woodpecker harvests an acorn or almond by grasping it in its bill, simultaneously pulling and twisting until the nut breaks free. The bird usually perches crosswise on a branch near the desired nut, and then reaches out to pick it. Occasionally I observed an individual hanging below a branch while harvesting an otherwise inaccessible acorn or almond. C. W. Michael (1926:68) wrote of a Lewis woodpecker harvesting acorns in Yosemite Valley, California: "Occasionally he picked an acorn from the ground; more often he flew into the lesser branches of the oak, and hanging like a great black chickadee he plucked the acorn from the cup." Once harvesting is completed, the bird flies with the nut to a shelling perch. The nut is carried near the tip of the bill where maximum gape is afforded. Although almonds with outer hulls intact are quite large, Lewis woodpeckers seem to have little difficulty in picking or carrying them. The bill does not always span the full diameter of the nut, but gape apparently is sufficient to permit the necessary purchase. I have seen birds drop nuts on occasion; they always retrieved them and continued to their shelling perches.

The shelling perch or "anvil" always is some relatively horizontal surface with a notch or crack into which the nut can be fitted. Once the nut is secured in such a crack, the bird proceeds to split it open and extract the meat. Each individual has one or a few specific anvils where it does most shelling. In 100 out of 137 cases observed at Livermore the birds shelled almonds atop their storage poles. In the remaining instances the tops of fence posts were used, or the forks between branches of the almond trees. When shelling at its storage pole, a bird perches near the top of the pole with its tail propped against the side and with its feet just at the lip so that the claws of toes two and three are hooked over the upper edge. This brings the head and upper body close to the nut, which already is fitted into a notch on top of the pole. The bird hammers in groups of three to five blows, with slight pauses between each group. Blows are slow and determined, unlike the rapid chiseling or scaling of *Dendrocopos* or *Picoides*. The body rocks back and forth at the hip joint during blow delivery, but the head and neck also move in relation to the body, directing the bill so that it strikes the nut from above. This technique differs from the usual woodpecker drilling behavior in two ways. First, the bill is used more as a hammer than as a chisel, the force of the blows cracking the nut open. Second, the direction of blow delivery is more parallel to the axis of the body than would be the case if the bird were hammering against a vertical surface. The bird raises up over the nut, appearing to stretch to full height, and then drives the bill forcefully down into it. Hammering is more of an up and down movement than a lateral one.

Once the acorn or almond is opened, the bird may extract the meat and store it directly, or it may break the nut into several pieces and cache each one separately. Lewis woodpeckers store in natural crevices such as the cracks in power poles (pl. 6,*b*) and dead trees, or the checked bark of oaks. They occasionally may widen these cracks before storage, but they never dig individual holes for each nut, as does *Melanerpes formicivorus*. Law (1929) observed an individual Lewis woodpecker near Altadena, California, which occasionally stored acorns whole and unshelled in particularly wide cracks in power poles. After a nut is inserted into a crack, it is pounded securely into place. A bird often tests a piece of nut meat in several crevices before finding a suitable fit. The bird periodically cleans its anvil by tossing off the accumulated shells. The collection of shells beneath a pole used as an anvil is conspicuous.

In the fall of 1967, I timed Lewis woodpeckers storing almonds in the Livermore area for a total of 688 bird-minutes. Ten percent of this time was spent harvesting, 33 percent shelling, and 57 percent in actual storage of the meats. It should be pointed out that not all of this time was devoted simply to the accumulation of nuts. An individual often ate part of a nut before storing the remainder in its pole. The birds also spent considerable time working over their stores, moving bits of nuts from one place to another, and occasionally eating some. They persisted in this behavior throughout the winter, not simply consuming the stored nuts but also continually rearranging them. I examined almonds from storage poles at Livermore and found that the inner surfaces often had fungi growing on them. I kept some of these almonds in a plastic bag, and they decayed completely in less than three weeks. Movement of the stored nuts, particularly turning them, could serve to reduce this fungal decay by periodically drying the nuts' surfaces. Movement of nuts also is important in keeping the store intact. As some pieces are removed and eaten, others are loosened. The birds move these loose pieces to new localities and hammer them into place.

In an average storing bout (n = 137), harvesting lasted 31 seconds, shelling 99 seconds, and storing 170 seconds. Storing occurred throughout the day, although more in the middle of the day than in the early morning or evening (fig. 5). In contrast, Law (1929) found that storage occurred mainly in the morning, with the bird he observed turning to flycatching in the warmer hours of the day. Flycatching was not particularly common among winter populations which I have studied, perhaps explaining why the storing and eating of mast usually continued throughout the day.

The propensity to store is not restricted exclusively to vegetable foods. S. W. Denton (in Bendire, 1895) observed Lewis woodpeckers capturing mayflies on the wing and sticking them into crevices in the bark of pines. Sherwood (1927:171) flushed a Lewis woodpecker from a fencepost and found that "wedged into the cracks of the post were several insects (some of them still alive) of the two species commonly known as 'salmon flies' and 'trout flies.'" During the hatch of carpenter ants described on page 31, the birds were not taking time to feed each ant captured to their young, but were sticking them into cracks in the dead trees. After the hatch was over, these birds began extracting the ants and feeding them to their

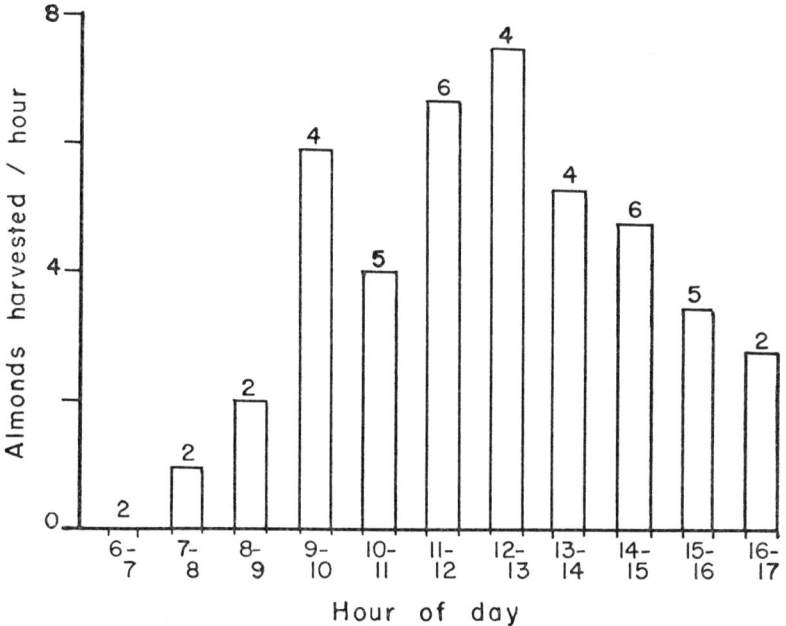

Fig. 5. Variation in the hourly rate of almond harvest by Lewis woodpeckers (n = 42 hours). The number over each bar indicates the number of sample hours in each time period.

young. Such behavior would increase the ability of Lewis woodpeckers to capitalize upon a temporarily superabundant food source by shortening the time between each capture.

Use of plant foods during the summer.—As discussed in "Habitat and Distribution," Lewis woodpeckers occasionally breed in lowland agricultural areas and feed upon various fruits or nuts, in addition to insects. Snow (MS) found this to be true for *Asyndesmus* nesting in the farmlands of north-central Utah, as did Neff (1928) for birds breeding in the Rogue River Valley of Oregon. It proved to be the case for the birds which I observed near Livermore. The bulk of this population consisted of resident birds which nested in sycamores and fed extensively upon green almonds in the late spring. Harvesting and shelling behavior were the same as in the fall, except that most anvils were located in the nest trees. There was no storage, nor did I see any evidence that the birds continued to use the almonds cached from the previous winter. They apparently preferred the green almonds of the current crop to the decayed remains of their winter stores.

The resident birds of the San Antonio Valley had no spring crop of almonds at their disposal, and the year's acorn crop was not yet developed when they bred in late May of 1967. Although the nesting birds did spend 11 percent of their time foraging over the acorn stores of the previous winter (table 7), these were very poor sources of food since the caches were virtually exhausted by the breeding season. In fact, nearly all of this 11 percent was recorded on 1 June, 1967, during the course of an unusually late and heavy rainstorm. The parent birds were unable to find insects to feed their young, and turned to their old acorn stores. Except in such emergencies, resident Lewis woodpeckers probably rely little, if at all, upon acorns during the nesting season.

In late summer Lewis woodpeckers feed on various fruits, berries, and seeds. Although I have observed very little of this behavior, stomach analyses by Baldwin (unpublished data), Neff (1928), and Snow (MS) indicate that such foods are taken regularly in mid- and late summer. Farner (1952) reports that migratory Lewis woodpeckers in Crater Lake National Park fed largely upon insects, but also took some currants, twinberries, huckleberries, and elderberries; one was seen feeding on a whitebark pine cone. Gabrielson and Jewett (1940) state that *Asyndesmus* competes with robins and bluebirds for mountain ash berries in the fall. At Livermore the birds fed upon grapes from nearby vineyards in August, September, and early October. Invasion of fruit orchards by migratory Lewis woodpeckers is widespread and has been discussed earlier (p. 21).

Summary of Feeding Ecology

Table 7 summarizes all of the quantitative foraging data which I have gathered from various *Asyndesmus* populations. The data for wintering birds were taken from Mt. Hamilton, the Livermore area, and the San Antonio Valley. There is an obvious shift from flycatching, gleaning, and ground-brush foraging during the breeding season to feeding upon stored almonds and acorns during the winter. Gleaning occurred more frequently in oak woodland, while flycatching and ground-brush foraging were common in the ponderosa pine forests and burns of the Boca Reservoir area.

A survey of references in the literature to feeding in Lewis woodpeckers shows a similar trend (table 8), although gleaning and ground-brush foraging are infrequently recorded by field observers, probably because these are less conspicuous activities than flycatching. Data for migratory birds are scarce (15 records), but the importance of seeds, berries, and agricultural fruits is indicated. Stomach content analyses by Baldwin (unpublished data), Neff (1928), and Snow (MS) show these same seasonal shifts in diet, from mast in winter to emergent insects in spring and early summer, with increasing numbers of berries and the like in late summer and fall. There is no evidence from stomach content analyses, literature references or my own data on foraging behavior to suggest that *Asyndesmus* ever digs for wood-boring insects.

A final point to be reemphasized concerns the opportunistic feeding behavior of the Lewis woodpecker. It has been mentioned several times in this section that these birds do not forage in a random fashion, but concentrate upon temporarily abundant insect populations. The birds breeding in the San Antonio Valley showed this particularly well. I visited the study area on five occasions during the fledging period in 1967. On 25 May, 1967, a large species of cranefly (*Tipulidae*) was very common in the grassland openings in the oak woodland. The Lewis woodpeckers were taking these flies by means of short, hovering hawking flights just over the grass. On 1 June, 1967, a heavy rainstorm forced the birds to turn to

TABLE 8
NUMBERS OF PUBLISHED REFERENCES TO *Asyndesmus* FEEDING BEHAVIOR

	Breeding	Winter	Migration
Flycatching	23(60.5%)	13(33.3%)	6(22.2%)
Ground-brush foraging	8(21.1%)	0	1(3.7%)
Gleaning	1(2.6%)	1(2.6%)	1(3.7%)
Acorns	0	16(41.0%)	2(7.4%)
Agricultural fruits and nuts	6(15.8%)	9(23.1%)	9(33.4%)
Seeds and berries	0	0	8(29.6%)
Total number of entries	38(100%)	39(100%)	27(100%)
Total number of references*	32	29	15

* In compiling this table, a publication referring to more than one feeding activity was tabulated under each category mentioned.

ground foraging and working old acorn stores. No insects were particularly abundant on this date, but one week later coccinellid larvae hatched in the grass. The birds took these by ground foraging. On 15 June, 1967, small unidentified flying insects emerged from the oak foliage, and the Lewis woodpeckers took these on short hawking flights over the trees. Finally, on 22 June, 1967, large numbers of ants were moving over the oak trees, and the birds gleaned extensively for them. These were not the only insects taken on the various dates discussed here, but the birds definitely concentrated upon these abundant species.

COMPARISON WITH OTHER WOODPECKERS

Several North American woodpeckers show patterns of feeding ecology similar to *Asyndesmus*. The acorn woodpecker (*Melanerpes formicivorus*), a resident of oak woodland in the West, is a flycatcher and also stores acorns in the fall (Ritter, 1938). Beal (1911) found no evidence that it ever takes wood-boring larvae. Unlike *Asyndesmus*, this species is highly social. A group of birds cooperate to amass large numbers of acorns in a power pole or dead tree. These social units apparently remain intact all year, although the status and function of the various members during the breeding season remains unclear (Ritter, op. cit., cf. Wynne-Edwards, 1962). Leach (1925) observed seven birds attending one nest near Walnut Creek, California; such communal nesting appears to be common.

The storage technique of *Melanerpes formicivorus* differs from that of the Lewis woodpecker in that acorns usually are stored intact and unshelled. Also, the birds dig individual holes for many of the nuts stored, in addition to using natural cracks. Apparently acorn woodpeckers can evaluate the size of objects to be stored;

Ritter (op. cit.) found that each acorn closely fits its hole. The hoarding tendency is so strong that acorn woodpeckers sometimes store pebbles (Ritter, p. 128); this probably occurs when acorn crops are poor (see Kilham, 1963:234). In the Capay Valley and at Livermore I have seen acorn woodpeckers storing almonds. The birds removed only the outer hulls, and stored the remainder intact in holes excavated to the proper size.

Apparently *Melanerpes formicivorous* relies upon acorn stores all year, as Neff (1928) found mast in the stomachs of some birds collected every month. In this sense it is much more closely tied to oaks than *Asyndesmus,* which usually is strictly a winter resident of oak woodland, with stores lasting only through the winter months. Ritter (op. cit.) found that for certain colonies of acorn woodpeckers the stores were so extensive that they appeared to be undiminished at the time of the next acorn crop. Oak woodland may be unsuitable nesting habitat for *Asyndesmus* because of the lack of insects during summer droughts. Acorn woodpeckers apparently compensate for this lack by storing enough mast in the fall to sustain them in part through the next summer. In any event, the feeding ecologies of the Lewis and acorn woodpeckers differ strikingly in this respect. If *Asyndesmus* is a highly specialized flycatcher switching to mast stores when insects are scarce, the reverse may be said of *Melanerpes formicivorus.* Since *M. formicivorus* mast stores may last all year, the nuts would have to be better protected from decay. This probably explains the adaptive significance of the acorn woodpecker's storing unshelled acorns and almonds. The expenditure of energy in digging cavities large enough to house intact nuts would be compensated for in the protection afforded by the shells.

The red-headed woodpecker (*Melanerpes erythrocephalus*) of central and eastern North America also maintains winter food stores. It resembles *Asyndesmus* more than *Melanerpes formicivorus* in several respects. First, *M. erythrocephalus* is territorial in winter, each bird defending an individual cache of acorns (Kilham, 1958b). Second, the nuts are stored in natural crevices, and usually are shelled (Kilham, 1958a). Red-headed woodpeckers store a variety of foods, including beechnuts, corn kernels, and a variety of wild fruits (Hay, 1887), in addition to the usual acorns. Hay observed that the birds stored beechnuts whole and unshelled when there were cracks large enough to house them. Unique to *M. erythrocephalus* is the habit of covering over stored materials by fitting pieces of bark and wood into the cracks, apparently in an effort to conceal them from other birds and squirrels (Hay, 1887; Kilham, 1958a).

The red-headed woodpecker is much like *Asyndesmus* and *Melanerpes formicivorus* with regard to insect predation. It feeds mainly upon emergent insects, taking them by flycatching, gleaning, and ground-brush foraging; it occasionally caches grasshoppers and other large insects in the cracks of limbs or fence posts (Beal, 1911; Bent, 1939). *Melanerpes erythrocephalus* is something of a predator on vertebrates as well as on insects. Bent reports instances of red-headed woodpeckers taking the eggs or young of flickers, robins, titmice, nuthatches, chickadees, bluebirds, and swallows. Charles Aldrich (in Beal, 1911:37) saw a red-headed woodpecker "kill a duckling with a single blow on the head, and then peck out and eat the brains." I have never seen the Lewis woodpecker robbing nests, although Sherwood (1927) observed one eating an egg. Bryant (1921) recorded an acorn woodpecker robbing the nest of a pair of western wood pewees (*Contopus sordidulus*). However, neither the Lewis nor the acorn woodpecker takes eggs or young birds to the same degree as *M. erythrocephalus*.

Kilham (1963) studied the food storing of the red-bellied woodpecker (*Centurus carolinus*). Unlike the red-headed woodpecker in the same study area, *C. carolinus* did not vigorously defend winter territories or storage trees. Kilham observed some storing all year, although mostly in the fall months when poison ivy berries (*Rhus radicans*) and acorns were cached extensively. There is evidence that these birds do not cache nuts in specific storage trees, but may scatter them widely over their home ranges. Blinco (1923) observed a red-bellied woodpecker storing acorns in fence posts from 22 to 180 meters distant from the oak source. It seemed that only one acorn was cached in each post. Kilham writes (1963:227): "On 24 October 1960, I watched a male working . . . for eight minutes. This individual perched on a branch as it reached out repeatedly to seize berries, then pushed them into nearby crevices. He didn't swallow any until about to fly away. The above example illustrates the fact that *C. carolinus* usually used storage places which are readily available and require no excavation." It also illustrates the fact that this species stores randomly rather than concentrating on one or a few specific sites.

Kilham (1963) found that red-bellied woodpeckers inserted the nuts or poison ivy berries deep into natural cavities by means of their long and adroit tongues. The birds stored the small pin oak acorns (*Quercus palustris*) and poison ivy berries whole, but usually broke up the larger acorns before caching them. He also noted in a captive individual the habit of spearing acorns when carrying them. M. Brooks (1934) observed *Melanerpes erythrocephalus* doing this also. As discussed earlier, *Asyndesmus* always carried acorns or other nuts between the mandibles rather than by spearing them.

Red-bellied woodpeckers feed upon free-living insects such as grasshoppers and flies, and upon acorns, berries, and a wide variety of fruits both native and cultivated (Beal, 1911). In addition, however, they do take numbers of wood-boring larvae excavated in the usual manner. This fact, and the differences in storing behavior outlined above, suggest that *Centurus carolinus* has a feeding ecology rather distinct from *Asyndesmus*, *Melanerpes formicivorus* and *M. erythrocephalus*.

The golden-fronted woodpecker (*Centurus aurifrons*) also is known to feed upon various fruits, berries, and acorns. Although extensive stores have not been found, R. W. Quillin (in Bent, 1939:248) states that "this species has an odd habit of placing shelled mesquite beans in the nesting holes." A survey of references in Bent reveals that seeds, fruits, and mast are eaten by a wide variety of woodpeckers, including *Dryocopus pileatus* and most *Dendrocopos* in addition to the centurid and melanerpine forms. V. A. Alderson (1890:147) described an individual hairy woodpecker (*Dendrocopos villosus*) carrying "potato bugs" from a field to a large pine stub. Inside a hole in the stub were "over two bushels of bugs," with "their heads off and bodies intact." The tendency to cache insects, at least, may be more widespread than is generally believed.

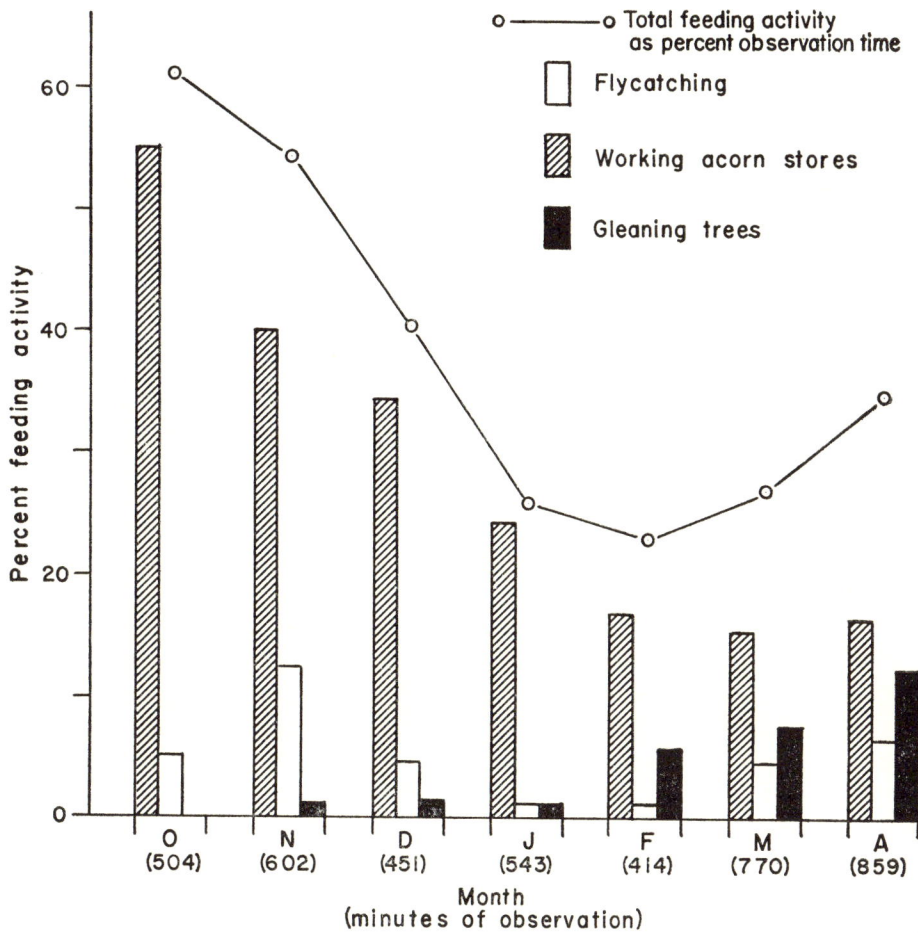

Fig. 6. Feeding activities of Lewis woodpeckers through the winter as percentages of total observation time.

If the utilization of mast and a proclivity for caching foods is common in the family Picidae, it is easy to see how specializations along these lines could have evolved in *Asyndesmus, Melanerpes erythrocephalus,* and *M. formicivorus*. It is certain that a dependence upon free-living rather than wood-boring insects is related to the accumulation of large mast stores for use during the winter months, when such insect foods would be unavailable. Without arguing for cause and effect, these two basic patterns of feeding behavior must have evolved simultaneously.

The Ecology of Acorn Storage

Time and energy aspects.—The storage of nuts involves a considerable expenditure of energy. One reflection of this fact is the total time spent in activities related to storage during the fall and early winter. Figure 6 shows feeding activity during the winter broken into various components and plotted as percentages of total observation time. This figure represents data from two winter populations. I timed the feeding activities of six Lewis woodpeckers at Livermore from October, 1967, to March, 1968, and two individuals in the oak woodland of Mt. Hamilton from January to April, 1966. These data combined show a definite activity pattern through the winter season.

Although I have no quantitative data for September, feeding activity seemed as high then as in the following month among the Livermore birds. Of 504 bird-minutes of observation recorded in October, over 60 percent were of foraging behavior. Ninety percent of this feeding activity, or 55 percent of total observation time, involved working mast and mast stores. It was not possible to determine what proportion of the timed behavior was spent in storage versus eating mast, since the birds usually ate part of each almond before caching it. Nevertheless, the decline in total activity obviously is related to a decline in storage activity (fig. 6). Activity remained low in January, February, and March, presumably because the birds had large amounts of food readily available and concentrated at their storage sites. The cached almonds were the most important food taken in these months and were obtainable with only a small expenditure of energy. In late March and April, as stores began to dwindle and insects also became more plentiful, the birds turned more to gleaning and flycatching. Total activity increased again as the birds spent more time foraging for insects.

The problem of excessive storage.—The Lewis woodpeckers which I observed in oak woodland on Mt. Hamilton and in the San Antonio Valley began storing acorns in September and continued sporadically into January. When the Mt. Hamilton birds migrated in April their stores were nearly exhausted. Similarly, the resident birds of the San Antonio Valley had scarcely any stored mast left when they began breeding in May. However, Lewis woodpeckers sometimes cache excessive quantities of acorns which they never use. J. E. Law (1929) studied an individual storing acorns in the cracks of power poles near Altadena, California, in January, 1928. The bird worked in the usual manner, hoarding large quantities of nuts. An inspection early the next summer revealed that (p. 237) "most of the acorns and acorn meats seemed to be still present in the cracks." Welch (1899:29) observed Lewis woodpeckers wintering in oaks near Copperopolis, Calaveras County, California, in December, 1898. Acorn storage was extensive, prompting Welch to wonder "why these birds store up so much food and then leave it for other birds to eat, for it is certain that they are not here to eat it themselves."

The acorn woodpecker also may store mast in greater amounts than would seem necessary for survival. Ritter (1938:25) contrasts a "Golf Course Settlement" (or colony) of birds, whose "stores are entirely consumed some weeks or even months before the new crop is ready for use," with a "Saranap Settlement" in which the birds stored so excessively "that, at the oncoming of the new crop of nuts each year, it is hardly noticeable that any have been used from the storage tree during the preceding months." Wynne-Edwards (1962:320–324) attaches much social significance to the fall harvesting and storing behavior of a colony of acorn woodpeckers. He sees the "acorn-rite" or "harvest-festival" as an epideictic adaptation involving competition for and assessment of the acorn crop:

On the one hand, competition is the means of applying stress, having potential consequences in relation to the social hierarchy, which can lead to the elimination of supernumeraries and determine the reproductive output of the community. On the other hand, the harvesting itself is a direct sampling of the food-resources on which the community must subsist until the following summer—the resource that actually determines the safety-limit of numbers.

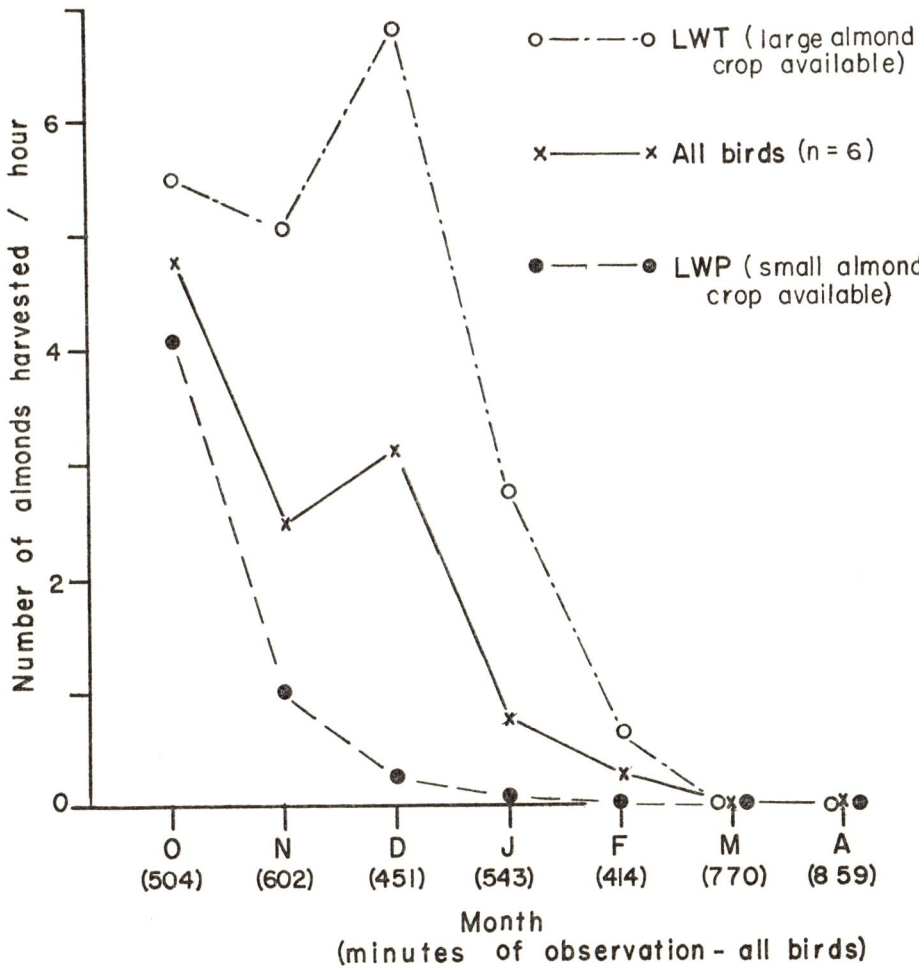

Fig. 7. Monthly rates of almond harvest for Lewis woodpeckers wintering near Livermore, Alameda County, California, in 1967–68.

Wynne-Edwards cites the frequent substitution of pebbles for acorns and the fact that only part of the acorns may ever be eaten as evidence of the ceremonial nature of this behavior. A part of his theory is weakened by Ritter's observations of pebble storage. The caching of small stones as "a direct sampling of the food resource" would lead to undue optimism on the part of the breeding colony. In any event, *Asyndesmus* is not social, and explanations for excessive storage must be found elsewhere.

The behavior of birds wintering in the almond groves near Livermore suggests that the number of nuts stored varies directly with the number available. Figure 7 shows the rate of almond harvest for six Lewis woodpeckers which maintained individual stores in that area. The decline in storage rates through fall and winter is apparent. This decline suggests that rate of storage decreases either as the mast supplies diminish or as the quantity of stored nuts approaches a given volume. The behavior of two birds (LWT and LWP) studied more extensively than the others points to the first cause (fig. 7). LWT wintered near a large almond orchard where little of the crop was harvested by man. This bird continued to store as late as February (fig. 7). The storage pole of LWP was near a smaller orchard where most of the nuts were taken by man. LWP stored only sporadically after mid-November, by which time nearly all of the almonds were gone. I attempted to estimate the number of almonds taken by each bird by collecting the shells beneath their anvils. This resulted only in rough approximations, since the birds shelled some nuts in orchards rather than atop their poles; also, because their storage poles were along a road, the shells which happened to fall on it were crushed by passing vehicles. Nevertheless, the differences were striking. LWP harvested an estimated 800 almonds during the fall and winter of 1967–68, while LWT took about three times that number. By late April, 1968, LWP had used nearly all of its store, while much of the other's remained.

Selection seems to have maximized the storage tendency in *Asyndesmus* without imposing limits upon the amounts cached. However, almond orchards are much more productive than oak woodland in terms of mast crops, and in this sense represent an artifact. Probably in most years the acorn crop is at a level where the advantage would be to the Lewis woodpecker which accumulates the largest store. Storing "too much" would be disadvantageous only if the individual could not obtain enough energy to sustain this activity; and since excessive storage occurs when there is a superabundant food supply (the extra-large acorn crop), energy demands could be met easily during this period. In other words, individuals which stored excessively might not be selected out of the population.

An additional explanation for the failure of some individuals to utilize all their stored food involves the possibility that mast actually might not be *preferred* food, even in winter. In April at Livermore, even those birds which still had extensive stores stopped using them and began to take flying insects and, particularly, green almonds of the new crop. It may be that the stored almonds decline in nutritional value through the winter from decay and desiccation. If a winter season proved to be particularly mild, larger numbers of insects might be taken, even at the expense of wasting some of the mast store. In the same way, a very large store could be a form of insurance against unusually severe winter conditions, and would be adaptive even if not fully used in milder years.

COMPETITION

INTRODUCTION

One indication of the importance of winter food stores is the vigor with which *Asyndesmus* defend them. It became evident early in this study that individual Lewis woodpeckers are extremely protective of their acorn or almond caches, driving all other birds away from them. This antagonism is most intense intraspecifically, but is also, at least in California, strongly directed against the ecologically similar acorn woodpecker (*Melanerpes formicivorus*). However, many other species elicit aggressive responses when trespassing upon a Lewis woodpecker's storage site. There are a number of literature references describing such aggression between wintering *Asyndesmus* and other birds. Perhaps the most remarkable of these is the observation of H. W. Wright (1908:93) who shot and wounded a Lewis woodpecker near Newhall, California:

> As the Lewis woodpecker lit on the tree trunk four California [acorn] woodpeckers attacked him evidently with the intent of driving him off. The Lewis started for another tree but a California flew at him from in front, and they both fell in the struggle that ensued. At this the other California woodpeckers, which were joined by a few more set up a violent chattering and when I ran up, to my amazement I found that the Lewis had hold of the California by the skull.... The Lewis woodpecker was dead and the California so nearly so that it died while I was removing the former's claws.

Linsdale (1936b) observed a group of 100 or more *Asyndesmus* near Butte Slough, Sutter County, California, and recorded interactions between these birds and flickers (*Colaptes cafer*), magpies (*Pica nuttalli*), downy woodpeckers (*Dendrocopos pubescens*), and acorn woodpeckers. Linsdale (1946:82) also observed a Lewis woodpecker attacking a beechey ground squirrel (*Citellus beecheyi*) which attempted to climb into its storage tree. This is apparently the only recorded interaction involving a mammal. R. B. Snow (MS) noted that *Asyndesmus* wintering in Utah defended their stores against other birds. I have observed aggressive interactions with a large number of species (table 9).

It is evident that Lewis woodpeckers are involved in an intense competition for food when accumulating and maintaining their winter mast stores. The concept of competition has been the subject of much debate, not only over its possible ecological and evolutionary significance but also over the scope and definition of the term itself. Birch (1957) and Milne (1961) have reviewed various usages of the word competition, both suggesting that it should be applied only in its strictest sense in modern ecological work. In contrast, Nicholson (1933) equated competition with any density dependent population regulating factor, while Darlington (1957:23) defines it as "the struggle for existence" and "any interaction among organisms that is disadvantageous to any of them," thus including predation and parasitism in the term. However, Birch (op. cit.) and Milne point out that Darwin (1859, chapter III) considered competition and predation or parasitism as mutually exclusive elements of the "struggle for existence." Milne (op. cit.:57) suggests the following definition: "Competition is the endeavor of two (or more) animals to gain some particular thing, or to gain the measure each wants from the supply of a thing when that supply is not sufficient for both (or all)."

Lewis woodpeckers defend their stores against all other birds which attempt to rob them. This is an unusual form of competition, since one of the two competitors already has possession of the resource in question. Nevertheless the two are involved in an "endeavor to gain some particular thing" (Milne, op. cit.) and can be said to be competing for it.

Lotka (1925), Volterra (1926), and Gause (1934) derived mathematical models predicting that competition between species ultimately will lead to the extinction of one of the two if the inhibitory effect of one population is greater upon the other than upon itself. Grinnell (1928), as a result of extensive field observations, concluded that sympatric species cannot and do not permanently occupy the same ecologic niche. The argument here is that if two species are required to share a limited environmental resource (food, nest sites, and the like), one will almost certainly be better adapted to procure this resource than the other and will thus eliminate the other (or force it to turn to other resources). This concept has been variously called Grinnell's axiom (Udvardy, 1959), Gause's Law, or, more descriptively, the competitive exclusion or displacement principle (Hardin, 1960; DeBach, 1966).

Orians and Collier (1963) point out that most evidence for competitive exclusion in nature is indirect. They cite five sources of this evidence. First, closely related sympatric species tend to have different ecologies (e.g., MacArthur, 1958). Second, closely related sympatric species may show character displacement, presumably resulting in a lessening of interspecific competition (e.g., Vaurie, 1951). Third, species often occupy a wider range of habitat types in depauperate areas such as islands, in which interspecific competition is reduced (e.g., Crowell, 1962). Fourth, there tend to be fewer closely related species occurring sympatrically than would be expected in a random distribution (e.g., Elton, 1946; Moreau, 1948). Finally, there are apparent logarithmic relationships between the relative abundance and density of species, suggesting that ecologic niches do not overlap (MacArthur, 1957, 1960).

A sixth and direct source of evidence for interspecific competition is the observation of actual physical interactions between competing species. Such interactions are not a necessary part of competition (two species may be using a common limited resource without ever clashing physically), but overt aggressiveness between two species, especially if they have similar ecologies, gives strong direct evidence that competition and perhaps displacement are occurring. Orians and Collier (1963) observed interspecific interactions between tricolored (*Agelaius tricolor*) and red-winged blackbirds (*A. phoeniceus*) in California, showing furthermore that the two species never occupy the same breeding ground simultaneously. They state (op. cit.:458) that this sort of direct evidence of exclusion may "be easily obtained in many bird groups," citing the work of Pitelka (1951) on competition between Anna (*Calypte anna*) and Allen hummingbirds (*Selasphorus sasin*) as a further example.

Asyndesmus is well suited to a study of intra- and interspecific competition in the field because of the high frequency of direct interactions related to cache defense. In addition, in California it is involved in an interesting interspecific displacement with the acorn woodpecker. By recording the number of interactions between resident Lewis woodpeckers and intruding birds it was possible not only to identify all competitors but also to quantify the relative competitive effect of the various species involved. Aggressive interactions usually took place when two birds met at the mast source (oaks or orchards), or, more frequently, when one bird attempted to rob the store of another. Thus, from the point of view of a wintering Lewis woodpecker associated with its storage site, it could be determined exactly what its competitors were, their relative importance, and the resource in common. Acorn and red-headed (*Melanerpes erythrocephalus*) woodpeckers are equally protective of their winter stores (Ritter, 1938; Kilham, 1958b), and data for these species should be applicable in the following discussion.

WINTER TERRITORIALITY

If we define territories as defended areas in some way related to food supply, then wintering *Asyndesmus* do not in this strict sense maintain them. Rather than defending a particular space for the food contained therein Lewis woodpeckers concentrate the resources (acorns or almonds) from that area in one place and vigorously protect that place. Most intra- and interspecific conflicts occur at or near the storage area. Figure 8 shows the locations of aggressive inter-

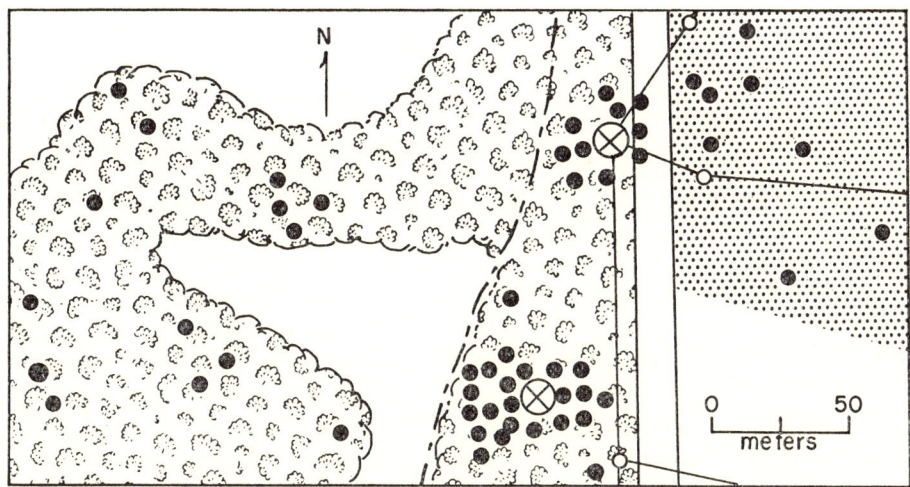

Fig. 8. Locations of aggressive interactions (dots) in relation to winter storage sites (crossed circles) of two Lewis woodpeckers which wintered near Livermore, Alameda County, California, in 1966–67. Stipple represents almond orchard; broken pattern indicates oak-sycamore riparian woodland. Small open circles represent power poles, one of which served as a storage site.

actions in relation to storage sites for two Lewis woodpeckers which wintered near Livermore in Arroyo Mocho, Alameda County, California in 1966–67. The birds clearly were most protective of their storage poles, although they occasionally pursued acorn woodpeckers, flickers, Nuttall woodpeckers (*Dendrocopos nuttallii*), and other *Asyndesmus* which moved through the area at some distances from these sites.

Wintering *Asyndesmus* were in attendance at their storage sites for 42 percent of the time (6,798 minutes). Attendance was highest in the fall, when the birds actually were storing acorns or almonds, but remained considerable throughout the winter months (fig. 9). Of this 42 percent, nearly half involved simply perching at the cache rather than feeding upon it. Such attendance undoubtedly serves to keep competitors away, as strange birds rarely approached storage sites except when their owners were not present. In addition, Lewis woodpeckers apparently watch their stores closely while they are foraging elsewhere; they often flew in from considerable distances to chase off intruders. The return flight was always rapid and direct in these instances, easily distinguishable from the slower flight pattern of a bird returning to its store under normal circumstances. The following are typical examples of such occurrences, taken from field notes of 24 October, 1967, and 15 February, 1968:

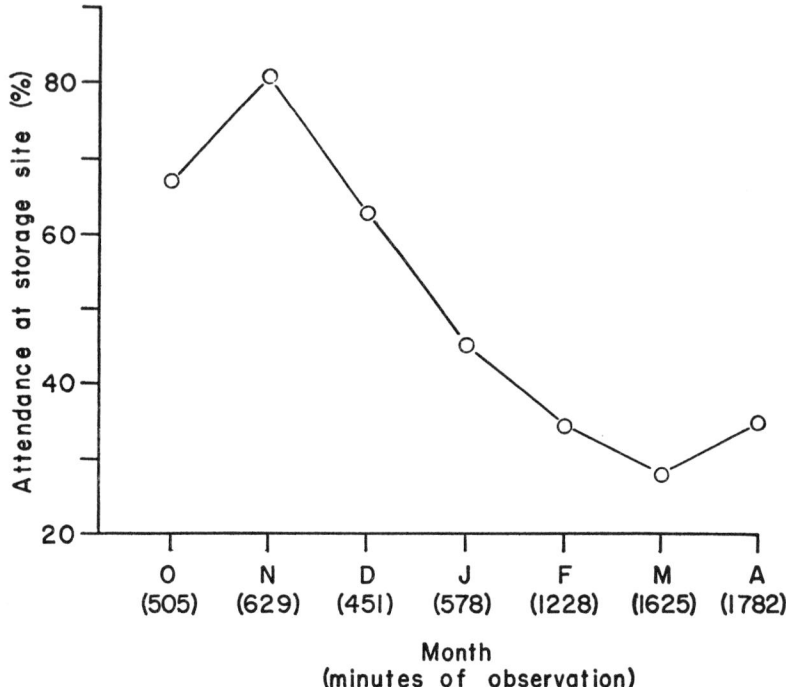

Fig. 9. Monthly variation in attendance of Lewis woodpeckers at their storage sites in the Livermore Valley in 1966–67 and 1967–68.

1309: Lewis Woodpecker T scanning atop pole T (its storage pole).
1310:30: LWT flies to the almond grove.
1311: LWT shelling an almond on pole back in orchard.
1311:30: An acorn woodpecker lands on pole T. LWT flies in and chases it 100 meters off to north.

*****

0958: LWP is preening in an oak about 150 meters east of pole P (its storage pole).
1004: A Nuttall woodpecker lands on pole P and begins gleaning over the stores. LWP has not seen it.
1008:30: LWP sees the Nuttall woodpecker and immediately flies in and displaces it.
1009:30: LWP flies to a nearby oak where the Nuttall landed and chases it off again. Then LWP returns and begins working stores.

In discussing the winter "territories" of *Asyndesmus* in California, the existence and distribution of acorn woodpecker colonies is particularly important. When Lewis woodpeckers migrate into oak woodland or almond orchards to winter, they must contend with already established *Melanerpes formicivorus* colonies. The result is an inter- as well as intraspecific spacing—not a continuum of defended areas but a scatter of defended points (mast storage sites). The distribution of these points varies with the availability and arrangement of potential storage sites and with the population densities of the two woodpeckers.

The simplest winter distributions which I have observed were in almond groves where power poles were used for storage. The use of these along a road through

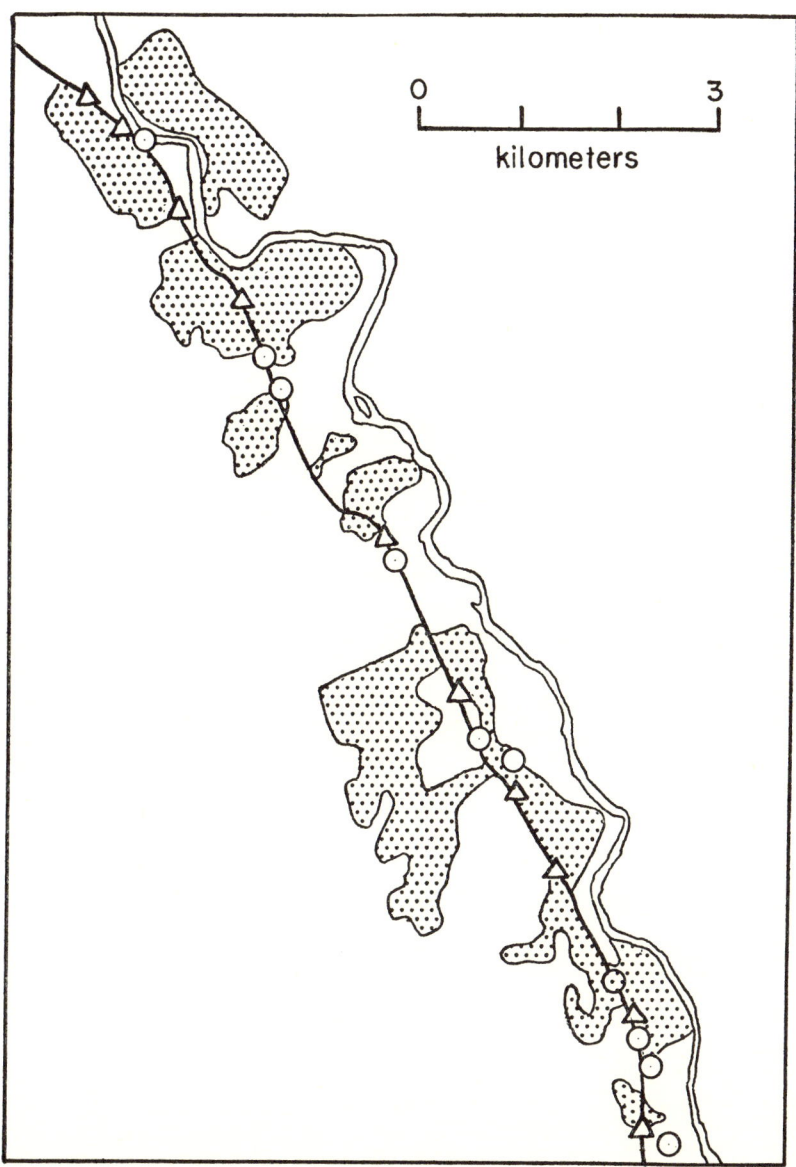

Fig. 10. Storage site locations of Lewis (circles) and acorn woodpeckers (triangles) in the Capay Valley, Solano County, California. Stipple indicates almond orchards. Power poles along a road were the most frequently used storage sites.

an orchard results in an essentially linear territoriality, as shown in figure 10 and plate 6,*a*. Each individual Lewis woodpecker or colony of acorn woodpeckers represented in figure 10 harvested almonds from adjacent groves on each side of the road, but moved along the road only at the risk of intruding upon another storage site. The linear arrangement and openness of this situation made it possible to observe several winter territories simultaneously, and to record all interactions between their holders.

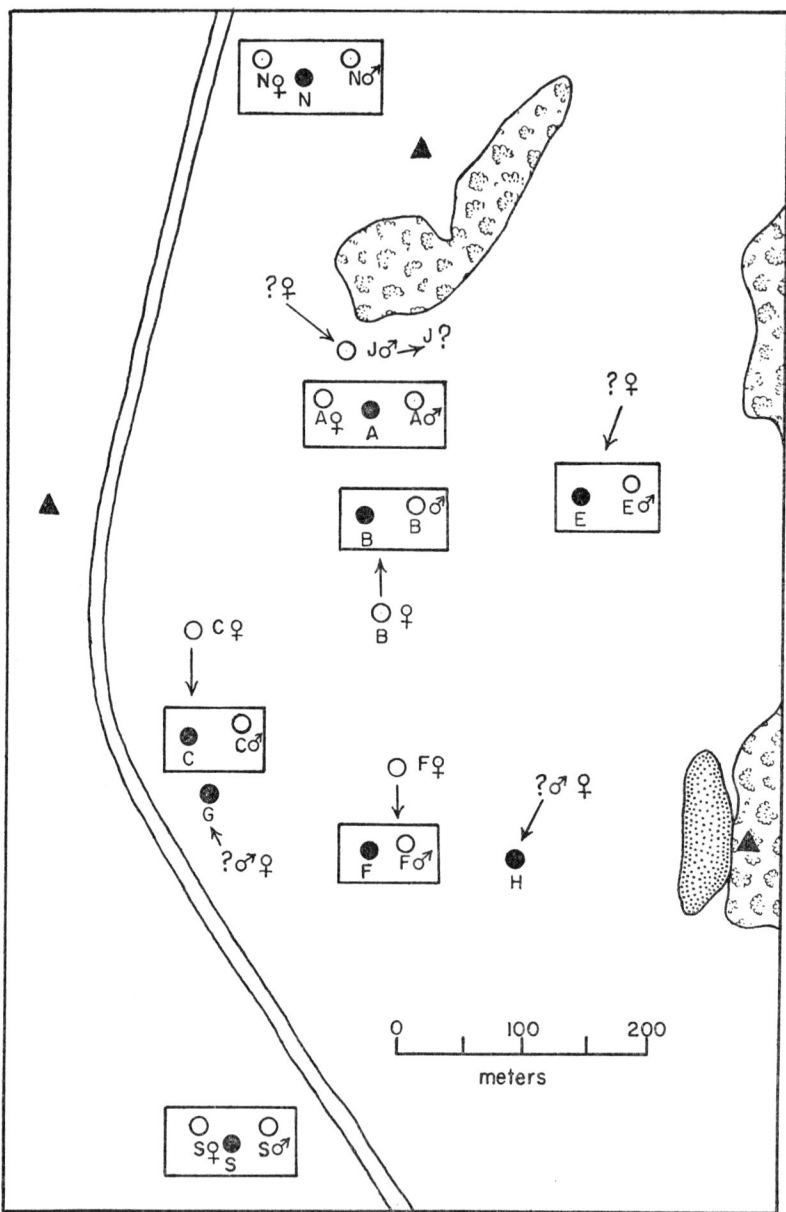

Fig. 11. Dispersion of a resident population of Lewis woodpeckers in the San Antonio Valley, Santa Clara County, California. Open circles indicate the locations of winter storage sites; closed dots represent nest sites; triangles are the locations of acorn woodpecker colonies. Boxes enclosing dots and circles indicate the use of a winter storage site as a nest the following breeding season. Pairs N, A, and S wintered as pairs and bred at their common cache trees. Pairs B, E, C, and F wintered closely but separately and nested at the male's storage site. Stipple indicates areas of pine, the rest being oak savannah.

In oak woodland the distribution of storage sites can be more complex. In the San Antonio Valley in 1966–67 I observed a small resident population of *Asyndesmus* more or less surrounded by three acorn woodpecker colonies (fig. 11). Six Lewis woodpeckers wintered as pairs at their old nest sites, while eight other birds wintered singly. Dead or partially decayed oaks were used as storage sites. Although this population was confined to a relatively small area (fig. 11) each bird (or pair) maintained its own acorn cache and defended it against all others of the group. This individual "territoriality" was less obvious than among birds wintering in almond groves for two reasons. First, storage sites were not arranged linearly; each woodpecker had more contact with the others surrounding it, making it more difficult to follow unmarked birds. Second, when the birds were harvesting acorns or hawking insects they moved throughout the range of the entire population. During periods of high activity the air would be filled with a confusing array of birds. Just west of pair A (fig. 11) was a low knoll covered with particularly productive oaks. All members of the *Asyndesmus* population, in addition to the acorn woodpeckers, flew there to harvest acorns; however, each individual always returned and stored at its own tree or stub. Aggression was high during these periods. There was much conflict in the grove itself; also, a bird returning with an acorn would frequently be harassed as it passed near another's storage tree.

At first appearance a dense winter population such as the one just described seems to be simply a loose colony storing nuts in randomly selected places within the range of the population as a whole. It is only after following individual birds for extended periods that the organization becomes apparent. Snow (MS: p. 51), who studied the species extensively in central Utah, found:

> Each bird does its own storing of acorns in its own desiccation cracks and excavations. There is no evidence of any kind of cooperation. However, as many as thirty to fifty of them will be found storing acorns in one canyon mouth in a very limited area. This storage area may not exceed two hundred yards in diameter and there is no evidence of semi-gregariousness. In the Fall and Winter no two birds store in one tree or pole, in fact, when accident brings two of these species to the same tree, limb, or cross arm of a power pole they are antagonistic and the intruder is worried until it leaves.

In contrast to Snow's observations, H. W. Henshaw (in Wheeler, 1875:398) briefly studied a flock of Lewis woodpeckers wintering in oaks near Tularosa, New Mexico, and reported that "within a comparatively small area, there must have been at least a hundred of these birds gathered together, and all combined to make a very happy, noisy, family party . . . . chattering as they chased each other about. . . ." This "chatter call" (p. 64) is in fact an aggressive note given by Lewis woodpeckers when defending their nest or storage sites. The density and activity of the flock gave Henshaw the impression of a "noisy family party," while in reality each bird undoubtedly was maintaining its own store of acorns, the extreme population density resulting in a high level of intraspecific strife.

Although I have never recorded winter birds in the density seen by Henshaw, I have observed several situations where storage sites were in very close proximity. A single Lewis woodpecker and a colony of four acorn woodpeckers shared a large valley oak (*Quercus lobata* Nee.) at a particular locality in the Capay Valley,

Solano County, California, in the winter of 1967–68. The *Asyndesmus* stored in a limb near the base of the tree while the *Melanerpes formicivorus* utilized several peripheral branches near the crown. I never observed an interaction in this tree, as each species kept to its own section. However, all individuals harvested from the same almond orchard and I did record a number of interspecific interactions there in the fall months.

In another part of the Capay Valley one large *Melanerpes formicivorus* colony and seven or eight *Asyndesmus* occupied a small grove of riparian valley oaks less than 100 meters across. The acorn woodpeckers stored in one dead oak in the grove while the Lewis woodpeckers maintained individual caches elsewhere in dead and living trees. Intra- and interspecific aggression was high here in October, when *Asyndesmus* had only recently arrived, but by mid-winter individual "territories" were well established and the rate of aggressive interactions had diminished. Birds whose stores were less than 10 or 12 meters apart remained mutually tolerant unless one landed near or flew over the storage site of another. If this happened the resident bird would give one or two "chatter-calls" as a warning, only displacing or pursuing the intruder if it did not fly off. Both the Lewis and acorn woodpeckers of this mixed group did considerable flycatching. On warm afternoons the birds executed long hawking flights, circling high above the oak grove. Although several birds usually were airborne simultaneously, often circling together, I rarely observed any interactions during these periods.

The behavior of this group and others like it suggests again the overall importance of the mast store. This is what the birds are protective of; there is no true territory except that of the storage site, and these sites may be in close proximity without causing undue social stress among wintering populations. However, it appears essential that storage areas be physically demarcated in some way, no matter how close they are. If two birds use the same oak, each stores in a particular dead limb. I have never observed birds sharing a power pole; this is probably because there would be no practical method of dividing it in half. An individual woodpecker apparently recognizes a pole, like a limb or stub, as some sort of physical unit. The one exception to the one bird—one store condition is the rare case in which a pair of *Asyndesmus* winters together (e.g., the San Antonio Valley, fig. 11). Here both birds store indiscriminately at the same storage site and share the cache with no sign of aggression.

There is evidence that Lewis and acorn woodpeckers will appropriate partially used caches if they are abandoned. The behavior of birds wintering on Mt. Hamilton, Santa Clara County, California, in 1965–66, illustrates this point. Two *Asyndesmus* held independent stores in power poles near Smith Creek Ranger Station, while there were two *Melanerpes formicivorus* colonies in nearby oak groves (fig. 12). In 1,396 bird minutes of observation prior to 26 April, 1966, the acorn woodpeckers made no attempts to rob the stores of the Lewis woodpeckers. Between 19 and 26 April one of the *Asyndesmus* (LWB) disappeared. On the latter date the other bird (LWA) was using both storage poles. In addition, the neighboring acorn woodpeckers moved into the area, resulting in five interspecific interactions with LWA in 281 minutes of observation. On 3 May, LWA also had left the area and the *M. formicivorus* were utilizing what little remained of both Lewis wood-

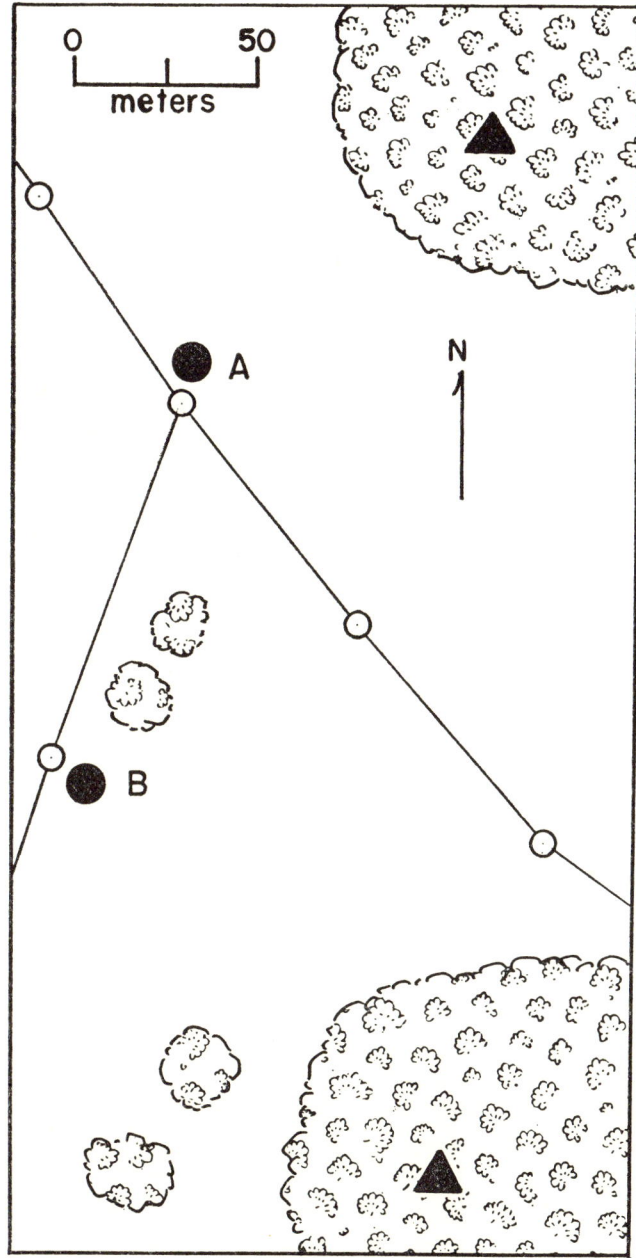

Fig. 12. Locations of two Lewis woodpecker acorn stores in power poles (dots) and two acorn woodpecker colonies in oak groves (triangles) on Mt. Hamilton, Santa Clara County, California.

pecker acorn caches. The behavior of these acorn woodpeckers suggests that there may be some advantage to Lewis woodpeckers which winter in groups rather than singly, since the former made an effort to rob the stores only after one of the *Asyndesmus* (LWB) was gone.

Proximity of *Asyndesmus* storage sites may result in a sort of mutual defense system, where the presence of one bird at its cache "discourages" competitors from entering the area where one or a number of other birds hold stores. One need not invoke group selection to explain this phenomenon. First, there would be selection for the individual to place its store near those of other birds; second, the protection of another bird's store would be the result of the defense of one's own cache. There are probably two opposing selective factors operating to determine the dispersion of wintering *Asyndesmus*. Increasing gregariousness would reduce interspecific strife through mutual defense, but would increase the amount of intraspecific aggression. Densities observed in the field probably vary with the degree of interspecific competition present in any given area—the greater the interspecific threat the more compact the population. Of course, another critical factor limiting winter densities is the amount of mast available to both Lewis and acorn woodpeckers. A limit to compression in *Asyndesmus* populations is the need for each individual to maintain a sufficiently large and identifiable acorn or almond store.

The unique colonial social system seen in *Melanerpes formicivorus* may represent one resolution of the conflict between inter- and intraspecific pressures. A number of birds amass and feed upon a common store, thereby reducing intraspecific aggression. Such a system also would facilitate the protection of the store against interspecific and "inter-colonial" competitors. The large number of individuals attendant at one site increases the probability that one or more birds will always be present to defend it. I suggest that the communal behavior of *M. formicivorus* may have evolved specifically as a means of protecting acorn stores.

Evidence for Physical Displacement between Acorn and Lewis Woodpeckers

It has been established already that acorn and Lewis woodpeckers show interspecific territoriality or spacing during the winter (figs. 10 and 11), but this does not imply necessarily any sort of active displacement. When *Asyndesmus* move into oak woodland or orchards in the fall they unquestionably compete with acorn woodpeckers for mast, but they might and probably most often do occupy storage sites which *M. formicivorus* have not utilized. In the Capay Valley (fig. 10) the *Asyndesmus* occupied power poles between established acorn woodpecker storage sites. The question remains whether Lewis woodpeckers ever permanently drive acorn woodpeckers from their caches, or if in turn acorn woodpeckers appropriate stores accumulated by *Asyndesmus*.

In virtually every instance of aggressive encounter which I observed between these two species, the resident bird or colony was successful in protecting and maintaining its store. The following excerpt from my field notes of 11 January, 1968, illustrates the attempt of three acorn woodpeckers to drive a single Lewis woodpecker from its storage pole near Livermore, California:

0846:30: Lewis woodpecker P leaves pole P (its storage pole), flies back into sycamores along creek.
0847:30: Three acorn woodpeckers land on pole P. LWP returns immediately and displaces all three, giving two "chatter-calls."
0848:30: LWP chases the three acorn woodpeckers out of an adjacent oak.
0848:40: LWP back and motionless on pole P.
0850:00: LWP now working over almond stores.
0852:00: LWP now motionless again.
0853:00: LWP chases off one of the acorn woodpeckers which flew toward pole P. Pursues this bird 60 meters north and lands on pole R.
0854:00: A second acorn woodpecker flies in and lands at pole P. LWP immediately flies in and chases this bird away, finally circling back and landing on pole P again.
0858:00: LWP still perched motionless on pole P.
0901:20: Third acorn woodpecker approaches pole P; LWP chases it off to the north.

This is a typical example of most of the interactions between the two species. They compete vigorously for unharvested acorns or almonds, and also attempt to rob one another's stores, but these interactions rarely result in any permanent physical displacement.

The only actual instance of displacement which I have observed took place on the Old River, San Joaquin County, California, in the winter of 1964–65. A colony of four or five acorn woodpeckers had accumulated a large quantity of acorns in a dead valley oak either during the fall of 1964 or in the previous year. When I discovered this colony in early November, 1964, two Lewis woodpeckers were making repeated efforts to rob acorns from this tree. However, the acorn woodpeckers were successful in keeping physical control of the site. On 12 December, 1964, I returned to the area and found the two *Asyndesmus* had taken over the store. They were removing the unshelled acorns, shelling them, and then eating part and re-storing the remainder. On that date the acorn woodpeckers seemed confined to a nearby oak grove. The two *Asyndesmus* kept control of this store for the entire winter, driving off the *Melanerpes formicivorus* which attempted to land at it. On 4 April, 1965, I observed a severe physical clash between one of the Lewis woodpeckers and an acorn woodpecker. Two *M. formicivorus* had landed on the storage oak when the *Asyndesmus* were away. One of them returned and chased off both acorn woodpeckers, following them in close pursuit. Suddenly the Lewis woodpecker dove onto the back of one of the acorn woodpeckers and both birds tumbled into the grass below. In a few seconds the *Asyndesmus* flew up and back to the storage stub, while the *M. formicivorus* flew off down the river. Neither bird appeared injured as a result of this encounter. The two *Asyndesmus* had consumed this entire store by mid-April, 1965, but remained to breed at the stub in May, feeding their young green almonds from a nearby orchard. It is unclear why displacement occurred in this particular case; but it seems certain that such an occurrence is rare and that most birds harvest, utilize, and successfully defend their own mast stores. The two species appear about equally equipped as competitors. *Asyndesmus* is larger than *M. formicivorus* and dominates on a one to one basis. However, the Lewis woodpecker is solitary while the acorn woodpecker is social, so that a competitive balance results.

The Problem of Coexistence of Acorn and Lewis Woodpeckers

Asyndesmus and *Melanerpes formicivorus* have strikingly similar ecologies. Although Lewis woodpeckers do winter in western British Columbia, central Utah, and along the Front Range in Colorado, where acorn woodpeckers do not occur, the major winter range is in southern Oregon and California, where *M. formicivorus* is resident. The question of coexistence arises. Two factors probably operate to permit the extensive sympatry. First, while acorn and Lewis woodpeckers have nearly identical energy requirements in winter, there are important differences in habitat and feeding behavior during the breeding season. Most *Asyndesmus* in California return to breed in the Sierra Nevada or Cascade Range, relying upon populations of free-living insects for food. The *M. formicivorus* remain to breed in oak woodland; here they not only feed upon emergent insects but, significantly, continue to utilize their large mast stores from the previous winter (Neff, 1928; Ritter, 1938). Even those Lewis woodpeckers which breed in lowland areas where acorn woodpeckers occur apparently do not have mast remaining in their stores by the breeding season (e.g., the San Antonio Valley population) and feed almost exclusively upon insects. There is a basic difference in the feeding ecologies of the two species even when they are permanently sympatric.

Slobodkin (1964:127) states: "If two species are simultaneously occupying a spatial region in which there is a broad area of ecological overlap—and hence we might expect the Gause situation of species competition to be realized—and if this environment favors first one species and then the other . . . , it is quite likely that a permanent nonequilibrium situation will occur." In a special sense this condition may apply to Lewis and acorn woodpeckers. If it is a particularly good year for acorns this would benefit *Melanerpes formicivorus* more than *Asyndesmus*, because the former utilize mast year round. If, on the other hand, there are numerous and significant outbreaks of emergent insects in a given breeding season then the reproductive advantage would be to *Asyndesmus*—the more specialized flycatcher of the two. Thus, even if the winter period is critical energetically, the competitive advantage may vary from year to year when the two species "come together" physically and ecologically in the fall.

Another factor very likely facilitating coexistence is the high degree of opportunism shown by Lewis woodpeckers. While *Melanerpes formicivorus* are permanent residents, *Asyndesmus* are sporadic and unpredictable, selecting wintering areas where acorn crops are especially large. In every area in which I have observed wintering Lewis woodpeckers they have been outnumbered by the acorn woodpeckers present. *Melanerpes formicivorus* is exceedingly abundant in California while *Asyndesmus* is relatively rare. The latter may be successful only in so far as it is better adapted to concentrate opportunistically in areas where acorn production has been unusually high for a given year. Hutchinson (1951: 575) has observed "that species, not obviously associated with successional stages on a large scale, may actually be able to exist primarily by having good dispersal mechanisms, even though they inevitably succumb to competition *with any other species* capable of entering the same niche." Hutchinson has named these "fugitive species" which "will enjoy freedom from competition so long as small statistical fluctuations in the environment give it a refuge into which it can run from competition." *Asyndesmus* do not ever appear to be free from competition with *M. formicivorus*, but by wintering in those areas where mast is very abundant the level of this competition may be reduced to the point where coexistence is possible. The Lewis woodpecker may well be a "fugitive species" when wintering within the range of *M. formicivorus*.

ANALYSIS OF INTERACTIONS

Methods of observation.—Wintering Lewis woodpeckers are protective of their mast stores not only against their own kind and against acorn woodpeckers, but also against any other birds which attempt to rob them. Breeding individuals do not maintain specific territories but are inter- and intraspecifically defensive of their nest sites, and do react aggressively toward other birds encountered in foraging areas. I recorded rates of interaction from the point of view of resident *Asyndesmus*. That is, a particular bird was observed at and around its storage or nest tree for a certain length of time, and all intra- or interspecific interactions were recorded. Data on rates of interactions were gathered from breeding populations at Boca Reservoir and the San Antonio Valley, while wintering birds were studied at Livermore, the San Antonio Valley, and Mt. Hamilton.

Resident birds were always dominant in interactions and successful in defending their mast stores or nest sites. Lewis woodpeckers drove off encroaching acorn woodpeckers, but were in turn expelled when they approached the storage localities of acorn woodpecker colonies (see p. 57 for one exception).

The *Asyndesmus* which I studied reacted more strongly to the presence of some species than to others. Simply recording interaction rates does not give a complete assessment of the relative importance of the various species encountered. In table 9 I have listed each species as belonging to one of three categories based upon the level of aggression which they elicited when trespassing upon or near a Lewis woodpecker's storage site. The following is an explanation of these three categories:

Intensity Factor 1: intruder usually displaced from anywhere near nest or cache and then pursued in flight until some distance from the interaction site.

Intensity Factor 2: intruder usually displaced from general vicinity of storage-nest tree, but rarely pursued and when so, only for short distances.

Intensity Factor 3: intruder displaced only when directly at the nest or storage site, and never pursued from that point.

Variation in winter.—In 6785 bird-minutes of observation I have recorded 146 aggressive interactions between wintering *Asyndesmus* and other birds—an average of 1.29 per hour. Analysis of data for birds wintering near Livermore in 1966–67 and 1967–68 suggests that this interaction rate is not constant (fig. 13). These data indicate a higher level of intra- and interspecific strife during January and February than in the fall or spring. Lewis woodpeckers were no more aggressive toward intruders during these months, but the number of encounters was much higher. This was tested statistically by breaking the data for each month into the periods of observation which were combined to give the monthly

TABLE 9
Rates of Aggressive Interactions

Species (intensity factor)*	Breeding-Pine Forest (7132 minutes)		Breeding-Oak Woodland (3544 minutes)		Winter (6785 minutes)	
	Number of interactions	Rate/hour	Number of interactions	Rate/hour	Number of interactions	Rate/hour
Sparrow hawk (†) *Falco sparverius*	21	0.180			6	0.053
Red-shafter flicker (2) *Colaptes cafer*	4	0.033	3	0.051	14	0.124
Lewis woodpecker (1) *Asyndesmus lewis*	25	0.211	11	0.186	26	0.230
Acorn woodpecker (1) *Melanerpes formicivorus*			12	0.203	43	0.381
Yellow-bellied sapsucker (2) *Sphyrapicus varius*					7	0.062
Nuttall woodpecker (2) *Dendrocopos nuttallii*			3	0.051	14	0.124
Western wood pewee (3) *Contopus sordidulus*	2	0.017				
Tree swallow (3) *Iridoprocne bicolor*	2	0.017				
Swallow sp. (3)			2	0.034		
Steller jay (3) *Cyanocitta stelleri*	1	0.008				
Scrub jay (3) *Aphelocoma coerulescens*					8	0.071
Yellow-billed magpie (3) *Pica nuttalli*					1	0.009
Plain titmouse (3) *Parus inornatus*			18	0.035	16	0.142
White-breasted nuthatch (3) *Sitta carolinensis*			5	0.085	3	0.027
Mockingbird (3) *Mimus polyglottos*					1	0.009
Western bluebird (3) *Sialia mexicana*					1	0.009
Mountain bluebird (3) *Sialia currucoides*	1	0.008				
Starling (3)‡ *Sturnus vulgaris*			14‡	0.237	2‡	0.017
Red-winged blackbird (3) *Agelaius phoenicius*	1	0.008				
House finch (3) *Carpodacus mexicanus*					4	0.035
Brewer sparrow (3) *Spizella breweri*	1	0.008				
White-crowned sparrow (3) *Zonotrichia leucophrys*					2	0.017
Totals	58	0.490	57	0.966	146	1.293

* Indicates the rigor of aggressive responses by *Asyndesmus* to the species in question (see text).
† Strong reaction to sparrow hawks due to threat of predation (p. 72).
‡ Not included in totals.

averages seen in figure 13. The data for January and February represent a total of 16 such periods ranging from 20 to 120 minutes in length. Rates for October through December, and March and April, were taken from 34 periods of similar lengths. The average number of aggressive encounters per hour in January and February was significantly higher ($\alpha = .05$) than the number in the months preceding and following, using the "t" test for differences of means.

From the point of view of energetics, the acorn/almond store is most important

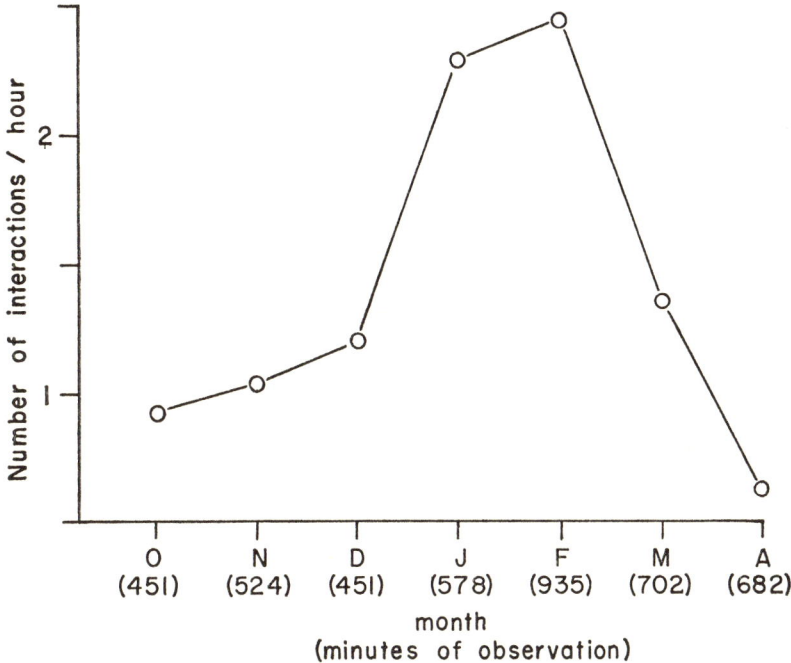

Fig. 13. Monthly variation in rates of intra- and interspecific interactions involving Lewis woodpeckers defending their mast stores.

during January and February (fig. 6). There is little if any mast remaining unharvested in the oak groves or orchards, and the spring emergence of free-living insects has not yet begun. Not only are the Lewis woodpeckers particularly dependent upon their stores during these two months, but presumably this would be a critical period for their competitors. Although I have no quantitative data, a considerable proportion of the energy available to the avifauna as a whole probably is tied up in *Asyndesmus* and *Melanerpes formicivorus* stores at this time. It is significant that while *Asyndesmus* spend the least time in feeding activities in January and February (fig. 6), this is somewhat compensated for by the greater amount of time spent in cache defense (fig. 13).

Seasonal and geographic variation.—Table 9 shows the number and hourly frequency of aggressive interactions between Lewis woodpeckers and other birds recorded during the breeding seasons at Boca Reservoir and the San Antonio Valley, and from various winter populations studied. A total of 277 interactions were recorded in 17,461 bird-minutes of observation. In comparing totals for the different areas, interactions with the introduced starling (*Sturnus vulgaris*) were not included.

Although the level of intraspecific strife remained relatively constant, interspecific interactions were much more numerous among birds breeding in the oak woodland of the San Antonio Valley in 1967 than for the population breeding in open pine and burned forest near Boca Reservoir in the years 1965–68 (table 9). There are several possible explanations for this. First, nest sites may have been in short supply in the San Antonio Valley, while at Boca there were numerous dead trees, most with unused holes in them. Breeding Lewis woodpeckers are particularly defensive of their nests, and it seems likely that competition for nest sites was more severe in the oak woodland area. Significantly, all interactions observed during the breeding season in the San Antonio Valley involved hole-nesting species (table 9).

A further explanation for the higher interaction rates in the San Antonio Valley lies in the fact that in this rare instance the Lewis woodpeckers were resident, nesting at or near their winter storage sites. (fig. 11). There was still a small quantity of mast remaining in the stores and many of the recorded interactions took place at one of these former caches. *Asyndesmus* remained protective of their storage trees on into the spring, perhaps because some mast remained in them or perhaps simply as a behavior pattern residual from the winter. Individuals of this resident population re-used the same trees for caching acorns in the fall of 1967 which they had held the previous winter. It seems that the birds here maintained a year-round attachment to their storage sites.

Finally, there seemed to be more birds, in both number and kind, in the oak woodland than in pine forest with which the *Asyndesmus* might be competing. For example, nearly two-thirds of the interspecific encounters in the San Antonio Valley were with the ecologically similar acorn woodpecker or the abundant plain titmouse, two species which do not occur in the eastern Sierra Nevada.

Rates of interspecific interactions were higher during the winter than during the breeding season in either area (table 9). The rate of 0.49 interactions per hour at Boca Reservoir actually is high as an index of competition, due to the inclusion of encounters with sparrow hawks in this figure. Lewis woodpeckers and sparrow hawks probably do compete for nest holes and for large insect food items, but in addition the sparrow hawk preys upon recently fledged woodpeckers (Snow, MS; personal observation). *Asyndesmus* reacts to this species not only as a competitor but also in defense of its young.

Although physical strife was greater in winter than in the nesting season, this does not necessarily imply more intense competition for environmental resources. The accumulation of mast supply may insure a winter energy source, but the defense of the store appears as important as its collection. Breeding *Asyndesmus* do react aggressively to other birds encountered when they are foraging, but the chance of these encounters is much less than in winter because there is no accumulation of food and thus no focal point for intra- or interspecific interactions. J. L. Brown (1964:161) noted that "defendability of the food supply, nest, mating place, or other requisites for reproduction or survival is one of the most important determinants of the system of territorial behavior which is attained through natural selection." Selection has favored individual Lewis woodpeckers which aggressively defend winter food caches because this behavior is functional energetically. Breeding birds are opportunistic, often feeding in close association in areas where insects are temporarily superabundant (see "Feeding Ecology and Behavior"). They are protective only of their immediate nest sites and do not defend a feeding territory due to the diffuse and sporadic nature of their food supply. The higher rate of interactions in winter probably is more a result of the unique kind of winter energy source than of its relative abundance.

Inter- versus intraspecific competition in winter.—In defending their winter food caches, the Lewis woodpeckers which I studied engaged in many more inter- than intraspecific conflicts (table 9). In relating this fact to levels of competition a basic assumption is that the aggressive behavioral responses of wintering *Asyndesmus* are adaptive and have been selected because they result in necessary protection of the winter food store, and furthermore that the frequency and intensity of these interactions is proportional to the ecologic threat which a particular species represents. The data shown in table 9 support this assumption since those species ecologically most similar to *Asyndesmus* also elicited the most intense aggression. Lewis woodpeckers reacted most strongly to the presence of their own kind and to acorn woodpeckers (Intensity Factor 1, table 9), the two being essentially ecologically equivalent in winter. In addition, *Asyndesmus* reacted more strongly to flickers, sapsuckers, and Nuttall woodpeckers (Intensity Factor 2) than to the various passerine species encountered (Intensity Factor 3). This presumably is because these woodpeckers were better able to climb on the storage trees or poles and to chisel into cracks for the stored mast.

In spite of variations in interaction intensity, the number of interspecific interactions so greatly outnumbered the intraspecific encounters it seems certain that interspecific competition was more intense than intraspecific competition in those populations studied. The frequency of encounters with acorn woodpeckers alone surpassed the number of interactions with other Lewis woodpeckers. I am not proposing that interspecific competition is the more critical for all wintering Lewis woodpeckers, or even a majority, but these data do suggest that such an occurrence is not unusual. The importance of inter- versus intraspecific competition obviously depends upon the relative numbers of each kind of competitor present. The point to be emphasized is that a Lewis woodpeckers's mast store represents such a readily available and concentrated energy source that a large number of species become potential competitors often to the point where they constitute a greater threat than other *Asyndesmus* simply because of their collective abundance.

BREEDING BEHAVIOR

Incidental to a study of feeding ecology and competitive relationships I have gathered certain information on the breeding behavior of the Lewis woodpecker. This is of interest first because, although *Asyndesmus* is known widely, few field observers actually have made quantitative observations on its breeding biology; as a result data on vocalizations and displays, incubation behavior, feeding rates, and the like are not available in the literature. In addition, the Lewis woodpecker is behaviorally and morphologically unique among the family Picidae in its specializations for feeding upon free-living insects. These modifications have influenced its breeding ecology and behavior in a variety of ways which are discussed in this section.

I have not covered all aspects of the *Asyndesmus* breeding cycle. Lewis woodpeckers become greatly agitated by prolonged interference at or near their nest sites, occasionally to the point of deserting them. Since the number of nests available to me always has been limited, and many of these were essentially inaccessible in tall dead trees, I have very little data on precise dates of laying or hatching of eggs, clutch and brood sizes, nestling survival, and other facts attainable only through continued and direct examination of nest cavities. According to my

TABLE 10
VOCALIZATION RATES FOR MALE LEWIS WOODPECKERS*

Season	Chatter-calls per hour	*Churr*-calls per hour	Drums per hour
Winter (5,739 min.)	0.32	0.00	0.00
Courtship (6,165 min.)	3.21	15.36	0.76
Incubation (3,405 min.)	0.83	1.82	0.05
Fledging (5,418 min.)	0.76	0.24	0.00

* Based upon 20,727 bird-minutes of observation.

limited observations and those of other workers *Asyndesmus* does not differ markedly from other woodpeckers in these characteristics.

VOCALIZATIONS AND DISPLAYS

Male breeding call.—Breeding male Lewis woodpeckers give a short, rather loud and harsh, *churr*-call, usually uttered three to eight times in quick succession. Bursts of calling come at irregular intervals depending upon the situation. If a strange bird approaches the nest site of an established pair, or if a female comes to an unmated male's nest tree, the level of *churr*-calling greatly increases. Rockwell and Wetmore (1914:317) describe a "rattling call" given in the spring, which very likely is the first description of the *churr*-call. This call serves to attract mates and defend nest sites, and thus is most common during the early stages of breeding. In addition I have heard males give it during incubation and fledging when strange birds approached their nests (table 10).

Lawrence (1967:18) states that woodpeckers have no vocalization "which can be said to function as a song or take its place"; instead, "the drumming of the woodpecker assumes much the same role as birdsong." Lewis woodpeckers seem an exception to this statement. The *churr*-call functions both to attract a mate and proclaim territory—the usual roles of true passerine song. At the same time, *Asyndesmus* drums very little.

Aggression notes.—Cooper and Suckley (1859) and Henshaw (in Wheeler, 1875) first described a chattering call uttered by wintering *Asyndesmus*. Henshaw (op. cit.:397) considered this a sort of greeting note given within a "family party."

Lewis woodpeckers actually give "chatter-calls" throughout the year, and most frequently during courtship (table 10). These notes are rapidly descending series of short squeaks. During the breeding season they often are associated with aggressive "wing-out" displays and "circle-flights" (pp. 65–66). I first considered the chatter-call a greeting note since males often gave it when meeting their mates during incubation exchanges or when both sexes arrived simultaneously to feed their young. However, these same birds also gave chatter-calls while defending nests and winter food caches against intruders, suggesting that this vocalization had an aggressive function. Davis et al. (1963:349) noted that the *"chrrp"* of the western flycatcher (*Empidonax difficilis*) had this same apparently dual purpose. They observed, however, that there was in fact considerable antagonism between the sexes and that the *chrrp* note rather than a "greeting" was a result of this aggression. It seems likely that the same situation applies to *Asyndesmus*, in which the chatter-call serves as a general aggressive vocalization. During the winter I have heard Lewis woodpeckers give chatter-calls during interspecific encounters with acorn woodpeckers which attempted to rob their stores.

It is not clear how frequently females give chatter-calls, if at all. *Asyndesmus* is so nearly monomorphic that I have rarely been able to distinguish the sexes except by their behavior during nesting. In the breeding season I have never heard a known female give a chatter-call, although they occasionally gave an abbreviated form of it consisting of two or three single squeak notes in succession. Two known females in winter gave simple squeak notes in response to intruders, but sometimes repeated them rapidly enough that the end result resembled a slow chatter-call.

Drumming.—Male Lewis woodpeckers drum infrequently and almost exclusively during the courtship period (table 10). The drum is a weak, simple roll, occasionally followed by three or four individual taps resulting in a drum pattern similar to that of the Williamson sapsucker (*Sphyrapicus thyroideus*). Drumming and *churr*-calling occur together during courtship and nest site defense. Lawrence (1967) noted that the females of many woodpeckers also drum. I have not seen this in the Lewis woodpecker, although its infrequent drumming and sexual similarity could make detection difficult. I also have not observed "mutual tapping" in *Asyndesmus*, although this is a common means of male-female communication in other genera of woodpeckers (Kilham, 1958c; 1959a, b).

Alarm notes.—Lewis woodpeckers respond to disturbances at the nest such as the presence of hawks, deer, livestock, or humans by uttering simple squeak notes. This occurs only when the adults have young in the nest and not at all earlier in the breeding cycle. Alarm notes vary between the sexes, a fact which facilitates identification of males and females. The male gives a simple *yick* note while the female usually utters a double *yick-ick* when disturbed. The frequency of alarm notes increases as the pair becomes more agitated. After I had examined a nest one or both sexes often remained nearby for up to 40 minutes giving alarm notes, their frequency gradually diminishing during this period.

Displays.—Male *Asyndesmus* give two displays which involve exaggerated extension of the wings laterally and dorsally away from the body. In the "wing-out" display the bird usually perches on a horizontal limb, with the wings extended and the head depressed, puffing out the silver feathers of the throat and upper breast. In this position an aggressive male may approach an intruder either head-on or laterally so that the pink feathers of the belly and flanks are presented in full view.

In the "circle-flight" a male circles its nest tree in a smooth glide with the wings extended and held at an unusually high angle, again exposing the long pink feathers of the flanks and breast. A circle-flight usually terminates with the bird landing at the lip of its nest hole and *churr*-ing.

It is interesting that both of these displays are involved in courtship as well as in territorial encounters. When males fly to and land beside their mates prior to copulation they often give a wing-out display and chatter-call before mounting. After coition is completed the male may drop off the perch and perform a circle-flight around both the female and the nest tree. Since *Asyndesmus* is sexually monomorphic, the female of a pair probably at first elicits the same aggression as a strange male, being accepted as a mate as a result of her submissive postures. At Boca Reservoir in 1966, I placed a stuffed bird near the nest cavity of an already paired male. This bird approached the dummy three times, giving wing-out displays and chatter-calls. The stuffed bird, of course, made no response, and following the third display the male attempted to mount it and knocked it off the tree. Hinde (1966) discusses the general conflict in birds between courtship and threat, in which the female of a species may elicit attack, flight or copulation on the part of the male. Lanyon (1957) noted in the monomorphic eastern and western meadowlarks (*Sturnella magna* and *S. neglecta*) that behavior patterns related to courtship closely resembled those involved in territorial defense; he concluded that "sex recognition on the part of the resident male must depend upon an 'indifferent' behavioral response from the trespassing bird" (op. cit.:35). Lawrence (1967) noted that the female eastern sapsucker (*Sphyrapicus varius varius*) elicited an aggressive response on the part of the male during early courtship, even though this race is sexually dimorphic.

Coition.—Mating occurs in a manner similar to that described for other woodpeckers (see Kilham, 1958c, 1962; Southern, 1960; Lawrence, 1967), with the male gradually swinging down beside or almost beneath the female during copulation. True coition often is preceded by a period of reverse mounting, in which the female flutters over the male before assuming the usual position.

Discussion.—It is generally recognized that avian displays have evolved as modifications or "ritualizations" of behavior patterns originally related to homeostatic functions such as preening, flying, or feeding (N. Tinbergen, 1952). The drumming displays of woodpeckers clearly have arisen from the foraging behavior patterns characteristic of the family. In addition the males (and to a lesser degree the females) of many species have acquired bright markings on the head, throat, and nape. These usually are red, white, and black, and very probably make an individual more conspicuous when it is moving the head rapidly back and forth while chiseling for food or drumming. Kilham (1959a, b, 1960, 1961) and Lawrence (1967) have described displays involving wing extension or ritualized flights in *Dryocopus pileatus, Colaptes auratus, Centurus carolinus, Dendrocopos villosus*, and *D. pubescens*. Their occurrence in these different genera suggests that this type of display behavior also may be common in the family Picidae. With regard to the concept of ritualization it is significant that *Asyndesmus*, the most aerial of North American woodpeckers and the least specialized for drilling, shows frequent and elaborate flight and wing-extension displays and at the same time does very little drumming. Furthermore, the most conspicuous red coloration occurs not on the head but on the lower breast, belly, and flanks, where it is best exposed when the wings are elevated and extended as in the slow gliding flight peculiar to *Asyndesmus*. Many woodpeckers have black and white patterns on their wings and tails which are flicked rapidly during displays (see Lawrence, 1967). The Lewis woodpecker lacks both these and the usual jerky flight pattern of most Picidae.

TABLE 11

VARIATION IN TIMING OF BREEDING WITH ALTITUDE

	Uplands (n)	Lowlands (n)
Average date of incubation	7 June (10)	15 May (11)
Average date of nests with young	11 July (18)	5 June (16)

TABLE 12

VARIATION IN TIMING OF BREEDING WITH LATITUDE*

	North (n)	South (n)
Average date of incubation	1 June (10)	25 May (14)
Average date of nests with young	29 June (19)	24 June (17)

* All records in Oregon, Idaho, Montana, and South Dakota northward versus records from California, Nevada, Utah, and Colorado southward.

TIMING OF BREEDING

Lewis woodpeckers normally nest during May, June, and July. An unusually late record is that of Jewett et al. (1953) who found a nest with young on 29 September, 1917, at Fort Simcoe, Yakima County, Washington. Thompson (1900) collected an early set of eggs from a nest in the Salinas Valley of California on 27 April, 1899. The Boca Reservoir population which I studied nested in June and July (table 13), while the San Antonio Valley birds began incubating in the first part of May with all nests fledging by the end of June.

Geographical variation.—The difference between the Boca and San Antonio Valley populations suggested a possible altitudinal influence on the timing of breeding. To test this I calculated mean dates of nests in incubation and nests with young based upon literature references, unpublished field data, and personal observations for "upland" (pine forest, logged-burned areas) and "lowland" (oak woodland, riparian cottonwood-sycamore) situations. The results (table 11) indicate that Lewis woodpeckers breed between three and four weeks earlier in lowland habitats than in mountainous regions (significant difference at .05 level using a two-sided "t"-test for differences of means). On a latitudinal basis there is no such marked difference (table 12). Populations from Oregon, Idaho, Montana, and South Dakota north averaged less than one week later in breeding schedules than populations to the south (differences not significant at 0.5 level). These data suggest that *Asyndesmus* is more responsive to local conditions than to subtle differences in photoperiod with regard to the precise timing of breeding.

Yearly variation.—Since Lewis woodpeckers feed opportunistically upon emergent rather than wood-boring insects, selection would favor those individuals which could correlate their breeding with the peak of insect availability. This probably explains the marked altitudinal variation in timing of nesting. Similarly,

TABLE 13
TIMING OF BREEDING IN RELATION TO WEATHER AT BOCA RESERVOIR*

Year	Incubation	Fledging	Seasonal precipitation (cm)	Percent precip. March to May	Average temp. March to May
1964–65	6/15 to 6/30	7/1 to 7/26	63.6	13.6	4.3°C
1965–66	6/6 to 6/22	6/22 to 7/24	37.9	15.0	9.2
1966–67	6/22 to 7/5	7/8 to 8/4	80.6	34.7	4.5

* Weather data from U. S. Weather Bureau Boca Reservoir station.

the Boca Reservoir population seemed to nest at different times in accordance with local weather conditions (table 13), although such a correlation is not proof of a cause and effect relationship. Precipitation and temperatures affect vegetation growth while all three influence insect emergence. *Asyndesmus* nested early in 1966 following a dry winter and a warm spring. The winter of 1966–67 was one of heavy precipitation, with an unusually large percentage falling late in the season (table 13); breeding was also delayed. In 1965 both weather and timing of breeding were intermediate between the two following years.

PAIRING AND NEST SITES

Pair relationships.—There is evidence to suggest that *Asyndesmus* may pair more or less permanently, or at least show a strong nest fidelity ("philopatry," as defined by Mayr, 1963:670). At Boca Reservoir one nest (A) was used each year from 1965 to 1968, while seven others were used from 1966 to 1968. I managed to capture and color mark one pair (E) in 1966. These birds returned and bred at the same site in 1967. In 1968 the stub had fallen but the same two birds nested together in another tree less than 200 meters distant. For the other nests there is no definite proof that the same birds were using them each year. One possibility, that the previous year's young were returning rather than the adults, can safely be excluded. First, pair A in 1966 and F in 1967 failed to fledge any young, and still these same nests were occupied the subsequent years. In addition, I color marked nine young from three different nests (A, E, H) during the study; none of these birds was seen again, while unmarked individuals (presumably the adult birds) continued to use these nest sites.

The behavior of the resident population in the San Antonio Valley provides more evidence for permanent pairing. In three instances (nests N, A, and S, fig.

11) male and female remained together year-round, storing and utilizing the same acorn supply in winter and breeding at the same site in spring. A third pair (B) which nested together in 1967 maintained separate stores the preceding and following winters; however, they remained loosely associated with one another and bred again in 1968.

Both in the San Antonio Valley and at Boca Reservoir unpaired males behaved very differently from mated birds during the courtship period. Most males arrived in early May at Boca if not already paired then at least simultaneously with their females. There was little courtship among these birds. In contrast certain unmated

TABLE 14
VOCALIZATION RATES FOR MATED AND UNMATED MALE LEWIS WOODPECKERS*

	Chatter-calls per hour	*Churr*-calls per hour	Drums per hour
Mated males (4,638 min.)....	2.20	9.85	0.19
Unmated males (1,527 min.)..	6.40	32.10	2.51

* Based on 6,165 bird-minutes observation.

males were vigorous in their vocalizations and displays. In the San Antonio Valley, males E, C, and J paired one week to ten days later than the others, following a more prolonged period of *churr*-calling, drumming, and displaying. Table 14 shows the difference in courtship intensity between mated and unmated male *Asyndesmus*. Many of the solitary males at Boca Reservoir never paired. The history of one nest (F) is of particular interest. In 1966 a male used the site as a roost, calling and displaying vigorously but never attracting a female. In 1967 what presumably was the same bird returned and succeeded in attracting a mate; I observed copulation on several occasions but the pair failed to nest. In 1968 pair F returned and successfully fledged young. These data, though largely circumstantial, suggest that pairing may be a lengthy process for Lewis woodpeckers; however, once mating has occurred it appears to be relatively permanent.

Lawrence (1967:61), in a careful study of the flicker (*Colaptes auratus*), the sapsucker (*Sphyrapicus varius*), the hairy woodpecker (*Dendrocopos villosus*), and the downy woodpecker (*D. pubescens*), found that "all the pairs under study mated for life." Kilham (1959b) distinguished between a resident permanent pair of pileated woodpeckers (*Dryocopus pileatus*) and an unpaired male which drummed continually through the winter. Permanent pairing and nest fidelity appear to be common in the family Picidae.

Nest sites.—A survey of the literature gives the following data for nests of the Lewis woodpecker: heights 1.5 to 51.8 meters; 47 nests in dead stubs, 17 in live trees; 29 in conifers, 31 in cottonwood-sycamore, 6 in oaks, 2 in power poles, 1 in juniper, and 1 in a catalpa; depth of cavity 22.8 to 76.2 cm; diameter of hole 5 to 7.5 cm. Of the nests in the San Antonio Valley one was in a dead oak while the remainder were in hollow limbs of living oaks. Pairs F and N (fig. 11) nested in natural cavities where no excavation was required. Ten of 11 nest sites at Boca Reservoir were in dead ponderosa pines, the other in a hollow section of a living pine. They averaged 7.3 meters in height, with a range of 3 to 12 meters. I was able to examine three nest cavities in detail; the following measurements in centimeters were taken: hole diameter 7.5, 6.3, 6.3; depth of cavity 30, 38, 29; distance from hole entrance to back wall 13, 20, and 19. All nests had a layer of wood chips at the bottom of the cavity.

While many woodpeckers excavate new nest cavities each year, *Asyndesmus* apparently continue to use old holes. The birds at Boca Reservoir used the same sites repeatedly; in fact, the only new nest constructed during my four years of observation was that of pair E in 1967, the 1966 stub having fallen. The male did what little excavation was required to dig through to the natural hollow used. In the San Antonio Valley the birds used their winter roosts as nests. Sclater (1912) noted that Lewis woodpeckers in Colorado utilized both natural cavities and old flicker holes. This preference for using old nests rather than digging new ones, and the tendency to nest in natural cavities or dead stubs, relates to the fact that *Asyndesmus* is poorly adapted for digging in comparison with more arboreal species. Lawrence (1967) found that the hairy woodpecker and sapsucker preferred live trees for nesting while the less specialized excavators, the flicker and downy woodpecker, preferred dead trees.

Nest site selection.—At Boca Reservoir arriving males and females established themselves more or less simultaneously at their old nest sites, although the males did some courting at this time. Unmated males call and display vigorously from selected nest/roost sites in an attempt to attract a female. The circle-flight may in fact be a symbolic "showing" of the cavity to the female. The behavior of the San Antonio Valley population reveals the predominant role of the male in nest site selection. In pairs B, C, E, F, G, and H, nesting took place at the winter storage site and in the winter roost hole of the male (I was able to sex these birds by their behavior during early courtship and to determine where the males were living). Pairs A, N, and S wintered together, each roosting in a different cavity at the same storage site. At least in the case of nest A, however, the male's roost was the one used as a nest. I have no evidence of nest rejection on the part of female *Asyndesmus* although this could account for the failure of certain unmated males to breed, and perhaps for the disappearance of pair J (fig. 11) in the San Antonio Valley. The J male attracted a mate successfully but both left the area early in the courtship period.

Lawrence (1967:67) concluded from her own work and a review of woodpecker literature that "although the males most often seem to be involved in nest site selection, no hard and fast rule can be set for a given species." She found that the male flicker, sapsucker, and hairy woodpecker most often chose the nest site, but that the female downy woodpecker usually did so. She also (op. cit.) pointed out that the male more often chose the nest because it arrived earlier than the female and showed a stronger "excavation drive." Male Lewis woodpeckers in the San Antonio Valley showed little or no "excavation drive" but attracted females to their roost holes by initiating *churr*-calling and drumming.

Breeding territory.—As I have mentioned previously, nesting Lewis woodpeckers do not defend extensive feeding territories, protecting only the immediate nest site from intruders (Nice, 1941: type "B" territory). All but two of 36 intraspecific interactions (table 9) recorded during breeding took place when strange birds approached established nest sites. The lack of feeding territories may relate to the opportunistic foraging behavior of the species (see "Feeding Ecology and Behavior"). Lawrence (1967:46) found that flickers, sapsuckers, and hairy and downy woodpeckers defended "territories" in the immediate vicinity of their nests against all inter- and intraspecific intruders, while maintaining large and flexible "ranges" only against their own kind. *Asyndesmus* seems to have no equivalent of the "range."

Unlike the winter season when both sexes vigorously defend individual food caches, female Lewis woodpeckers are not active in nest defense. They usually perched silently nearby while the males chased off intruders with *churr*-calls, chatter-calls, and wing extension displays. On 20 May, 1967, I observed an encounter at nest D, Boca Reservoir, between a resident male and two strange *Asyndesmus*. After 45 minutes of intense vocalization and display on the part of all three birds, the resident male dropped upon the back of one of the other individuals while both were in flight. Thus locked together they tumbled about 15 meters into the brush below, both flying out unharmed a few seconds later. This sort of physical encounter was rare, as resident males usually were successful in defending their nest sites through display behavior alone.

INCUBATION

Clutch size and incubation period.—According to Bendire (1895), Lewis woodpeckers lay from five to nine white eggs, the usual clutch being six or seven. In surveying other published references I have found these figures generally accurate, although Thompson (1900) reported clutches of four to five eggs for birds nesting in the Salinas Valley of California. Two nests at Boca Reservoir contained six eggs each in 1967. Bendire (1895) found that Lewis woodpeckers incubated for about two weeks, while Bailey and Niedrach (1965) report an incubation period of 12 to 13 days. Snow (MS) concluded that incubation, from laying of the first egg to hatching, took from 14 to 16 days. Although I did not check nests to determine precise stages of egg-laying, adult birds showed incubation behavior for 14 days at nests A and B in the San Antonio Valley and nest A at Boca Reservoir (1966), and for 13 days at nest G in the San Antonio Valley.

Role of the sexes in incubation.—Male Lewis woodpeckers brood the eggs at night, while both sexes participate during the daylight hours. Males and females both develop brood patches. For seven nests in which I could identify the sexes the males showed a markedly greater proportion of attentive behavior during the day than the females (table 15). Kendeigh (1952) noted that in most woodpeckers studied the male sleeps on the eggs. Recently Stickel (1965) found this to be the case for the red-bellied woodpecker (*Centurus carolinus*), as did Lawrence (1967) for the flicker, sapsucker, and hairy and downy woodpeckers.

Daily attentiveness.—During the incubation period at least one adult was in attendance at the nest for 94 percent of 51 hours observation. Actual incubation only occurred for 68 percent of the observation time; for the remainder one or both adults were perched outside the nest, usually within a few feet of the entrance. This is in sharp contrast to the behavior of those species studied by Lawrence (1967:105) which incubated "not less than 95 percent of the time during the day."

Although *Asyndesmus'* attentiveness remained nearly constant all day, the eggs were covered a greater amount of the time in the colder morning hours than in the afternoon or early evening (fig. 14). Stickel (1965:115) similarly observed in the red-bellied woodpecker that "during the heat of the day the attentive adult spent more time outside the cavity than it did during the cooler parts of the early morning." In *Asyndesmus*, attentiveness and incubation both dropped in the evening due to increased foraging activity by both sexes prior to retiring for the night (fig. 14).

TABLE 15

NEST ATTENTIVENESS OF MALE AND FEMALE LEWIS WOODPECKERS DURING THE INCUBATION PERIOD*

	Attentive periods (minutes)				Inattentive periods (minutes)			
	n	$\bar{X}$	Range	% attentive	n	$\bar{X}$	Range	%inattentive
Males.......	84	25.1	1 to 115	69	76	12.5	1 to 102	31
Females.....	35	25.7	1 to 82	29	38	56.2	1.5 to 410	71

* Data obtained from seven nesting pairs.

NESTLING PERIOD

Fledging time.—Bendire (1895) reported a fledging period of about three weeks for the Lewis woodpecker. In contrast Snow (MS) found that the adults continued to feed young in the nest from four to five weeks. Although I have no precise data on hatching times, observations on four nests at Boca Reservoir and three in the San Antonio Valley indicate a minimum fledging period of 28 or 29 days and a maximum of 32 or 34.

Two or three days before the young start to fly they begin to venture out onto the nest stub and to climb about in an exploratory fashion. Snow (MS) observed in Utah that sparrow hawks (*Falco sparverius*) took many young at this time. He wrote: "As the young come to an open space in the branches, the Sparrow Hawks swoop from their perch(es) and pick them off the limb with great efficiency. The practice is to carry them to a nearby limb where they are eviscerated. In some districts the hawks may kill two to three young from each nest in this manner." Although I have never seen a sparrow hawk actually take a juvenile Lewis woodpecker in California, they frequently harassed young birds both at Boca and the San Antonio Valley. On 29 June, 1967, I discovered the remains of a recently fledged juvenile beneath nest B in the San Antonio Valley, where a sparrow hawk was seen repeatedly swooping past the nest hole seven days earlier. The behavior of fledged birds still being fed by their parents suggests an avoidance response to hawks. For example, a pair of *Falco sparverius* was continually harassing the adults and young at nest G (Boca Reservoir) in 1967. As soon as the young were advanced enough to fly they left the nest site—a dead stub—and flew into the dense foliage of a nearby living pine. The young kept hidden here for three days while the adults continued to feed them.

Adults and juveniles remain closely associated following fledging. In 1967 I color marked the young from two nests at Boca Reservoir. At each nest the adults separated, each taking a part of the brood with them. However, all birds remained in the general vicinity of the nest for about ten days. During this time the young at first followed their parents closely, giving begging notes whenever the adults

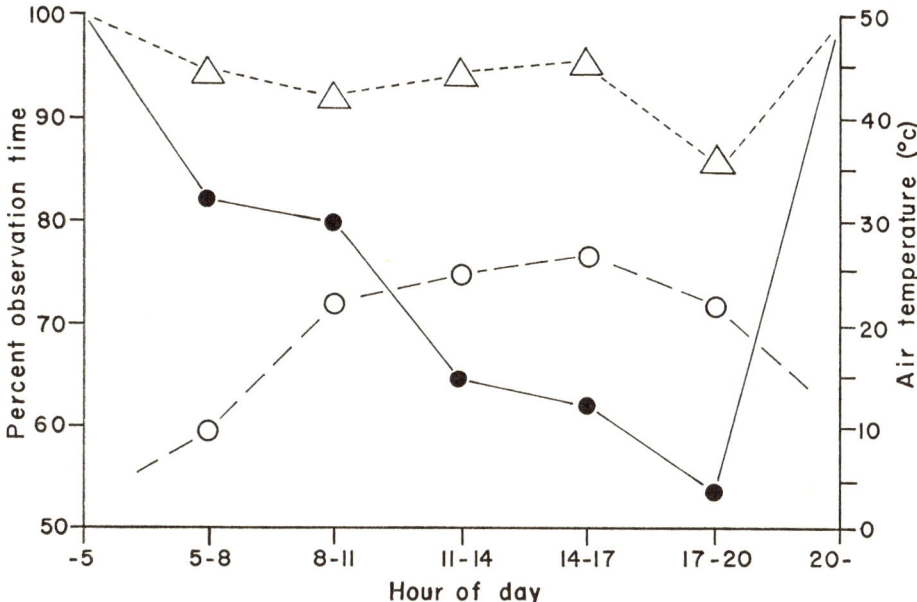

Fig. 14. Diurnal variation of nest attendance (triangles) and actual incubation (dots) in relation to an average daily fluctuation in air temperature (circles). (See text.)

approached with food. Gradually the juveniles began to forage on their own. On 15 August I watched young "learning" to flycatch. They flew in clumsy arcs, often tumbling several meters in the air while attempting to capture a flying insect, and also had difficulty returning to their hawking perches.

Feeding rates.—Nesting pairs of Lewis woodpeckers averaged 15.1 feedings of the young per hour (n = 110) with a range of 2 to 62 and a standard deviation of 10.1. This feeding rate is within the range for those woodpeckers listed by Kendeigh (1952). Lawrence (1967) found feeding rates varying from 2.2 per hour in the flicker to 14.8 per hour in the downy woodpecker. Stickel (1965) does not give an overall average for the red-bellied woodpecker, but shows a diurnal variation of 4.5 to 15.7 feedings per hour.

Kendeigh (1952:11) noted that birds generally are most active in the early morning and late afternoon and evening, with a decline in midday. This often influences the daily fluctuation in feeding rates. Stickel (1965) found that the red-bellied woodpecker fed more often in the morning and afternoon, in accordance with this sort of rhythm. Perhaps due to the sporadic availability of their foods (related to such things as insect hatches and hourly weather conditions), especially in contrast to wood-boring insects taken by other woodpeckers, feeding rates for *Asyndesmus* showed no marked daily pattern (table 16), nor obvious correla-

TABLE 16
DAILY VARIATION IN FEEDING RATES
(110 HOURS NEST OBSERVATION)

Hour (PST)	N	Average rate/hour
0400–0500	3	5.0
0500–0600	6	10.3
0600–0700	6	19.5
0700–0800	7	18.7
0800–0900	8	15.7
0900–1000	5	20.0
1000–1100	7	18.1
1100–1200	11	12.4
1200–1300	10	13.2
1300–1400	8	14.1
1400–1500	8	13.2
1500–1600	5	15.0
1600–1700	7	16.7
1700–1800	8	18.5
1800–1900	8	12.1
1900–2000	3	17.3

tion with the ages of their young. Adults fed an average of 10.4 times per hour during the first week of fledging, 19.7 the second week, 14.2 the third week, and 16.0 the fourth week. This is yet another example of the way in which opportunism has so strongly influenced the Lewis woodpecker's natural history. During the height of an insect emergence feeding rates often become very high. In the San Antonio Valley on 22 June, 1967, a pair of Lewis woodpeckers was foraging upon ants swarming in the oaks. Between 0600 and 0800 hours they made 114 visits to the nest with food. In contrast a heavy rain on 1 June so reduced the foods available to this same pair that they fed only 43 times in five hours of observation. Breeding adults may store insects in cracks in the nest stub during heavy insect flights, feeding them to their young at a later time. This was seen during the flight of carpenter ants (*Campanotus*) which occurred on 19 July, 1966, at Boca Reservoir.

Attendance, brooding, and nest sanitation.—Males brooded their young at night up until the last week of the nestling period, when both adults slept away from the nest. Diurnal attentiveness and brooding were high during the first week (fig. 15), when one parent was at or in the nest almost continually. The higher amount of brooding early in nestling life probably accounts for the lower feeding rates observed during this period. Stickel (1965) observed the same phenomenon in the red-bellied woodpecker.

In 4,459 minutes of nest observation, the adults were seen to remove fecal sacs only 18 times; they usually flew away from the nest site before dropping the fecal matter. Stickel (1965:116) noted that only male red-bellied woodpeckers removed feces and that "two cavities examined . . . became progressively more soiled with fecal matter, indicating that the adults were probably unable to maintain both the nutritional demands of the nestlings and sanitation of the cavity." Lawrence

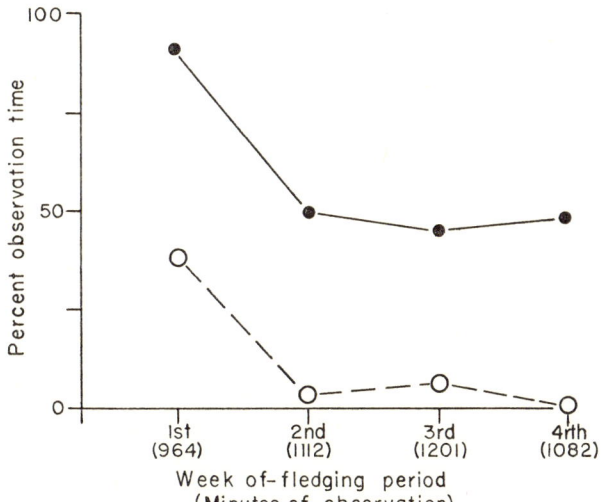

Fig. 15. Variation of nest attentiveness (dots) and diurnal brooding (circles) during the nestling period.

TABLE 17
ROLE OF THE SEXES DURING THE NESTLING PERIOD*

	Male	Female
Average feeding rate/hour	8.52	8.55
Diurnal brooding (% of day)	3.0	3.4
Diurnal attentiveness (% of day)	29.3	31.0
Broods at night	Yes	No
Removed fecal sac	7	2

* Based on 3,789 observation minutes when sexes known.

(1967) noted that woodpeckers often eat fecal matter rather than carrying it away from the cavity. It is possible that *Asyndesmus* do this, but I have not observed it.

Role of the sexes.—According to Kendeigh (1952:228–29) in the family Picidae the male usually broods at night and often is more active in brooding and feeding the young. However, the data which I gathered for *Asyndesmus* (table 17) suggest that males and females participate about equally in diurnal care of the young. Stickel (1965) observed similar behavior in the red-bellied woodpecker. In contrast, Lawrence (1967:117) found for the flicker, sapsucker, and hairy and downy woodpeckers that: "In general, the male's share in feeding the young is greater than the female's.... This is due to the female's preoccupation with brooding and defense, activities in which she usually undertakes the greater responsibility."

ASSOCIATION OF YOUNG WITH ADULTS, AND POST-JUVENILE MOLT

A post-breeding flock of Lewis woodpeckers which I observed in altitudinal migration in 1965 was composed of both adult and young birds. However, there is conflicting opinion in the literature about the composition of migrant flocks.

Cooper (1870) reported seeing groups of young birds in California, and Coues (1874) observed that the young seemed to band together after breeding in Arizona. In contrast, Nuttall (1840) and Newberry (1857) wrote of mixed post-breeding flocks in the Cascade region. H. Brown (1902) states that a group of *Asyndesmus* near Tucson was composed largely but apparently not entirely of young birds. Unfortunately, neither Adams (1941) nor Smith (1941), who observed migrating flocks of Lewis woodpeckers in California, made mention of their age composition.

According to Snow (MS), migrating flocks in Utah were "made up of mostly young and adult females with occasionally a few old males." The validity of this statement is rather dubious. First, it is extremely difficult to distinguish females from males; second, it is impossible to recognize "old males."

In the Central Valley of California, I have seen adults and juveniles associated when they first arrived on the winter grounds. However, as soon as the adults began to accumulate mast stores they became very aggressive towards these young as well as other adult birds. I suspect that the young then moved away to establish their own stores, but I have not been able to prove this since they began to molt into adult body plumage at this time and became indistinguishable.

Breeding *Asyndesmus* begin a post-nuptial molt before their young have left the nest; it apparently is prolonged, since certain specimens in the Museum of Vertebrate Zoology collected in winter habitat (as late as 10 November) still show stages of feather replacement. Juvenile Lewis woodpeckers have nearly completed a molt into adult wing and tail feathers before they fledge. Interestingly, they retain the drab juvenile body plumage until about the time of their dissociation with adults in the fall or early winter. This suggests that retention of the juvenile body plumage has evolved as a means of reducing aggression between adults and young. The silver collar and the red feathers of the breast, belly, and cheeks, seem to be acquired at the same time that the young birds begin to establish and defend their own winter food stores.

POSSIBLE EVOLUTION AND RELATIONSHIPS OF ASYNDESMUS

Garrod (1873) and Burt (1930) divided the genera of North American woodpeckers into two groups based upon certain morphological and behavioral features. One group, consisting of *Colaptes, Dryocopus, Melanerpes, Centurus,* and *Asyndesmus,* is characterized by having a semi-tendinosus muscle, a narrower skull, a narrower and more hooked bill, and by lacking a fold along the leading edge of the frontal bone on the skull. The second group (*Dendrocopos, Sphyrapicus, Picoides,* and *Campephilus*) lacks the semitendinosus muscle, has a broader skull, a broader and straighter bill, and a pronounced folding of the frontal bone. Burt (op. cit.) pointed out that this second group was much more arboreal and specialized for chiseling into wood than the first. Peters (1948) placed all woodpeckers into one of two groups depending upon bill morphology and the relative lengths of the third and fourth toes, and pointed out that North American species separated by these characters fell into the same divisions which Garrod and Burt had recognized. In contrast to these views, W. Bock (1963:278) has suggested that "... similar conditions of the foot, tail, and bill appeared three times within the family Picinae ...," and has proposed a rather different phylogeny based upon color pattern, in which, for example, *Dryocopus* is considered ancestral to *Campephilus*.

Whichever scheme has phylogenetic validity, *Asyndesmus* almost certainly is more closely related to *Melanerpes* and *Centurus* than to any other woodpecker genera. The three genera are similar in morphology and coloration, being less specialized for excavation than forms such as *Dendrocopos, Picoides*, or *Dryocopus*. Of particular significance is the fact that many *Centurus* and *Melanerpes* species, like *Asyndesmus*, feed to a considerable degree by flycatching during the breeding season and may store mast for the winter. To my knowledge, mast storage is not known in the family Picidae outside these genera. Whatever classification scheme is correct, the Lewis woodpecker almost certainly belongs to the New World centurid or melanerpine line.

The exact positioning of *Asyndesmus* among melanerpine woodpeckers awaits a much needed systematic treatment of the group as a whole. Peters (op. cit.) has lumped all species except *Asyndesmus lewis* into *Melanerpes*, while Todd (1946) argued for the separation of *Centurus* from *Melanerpes*. The genus *Centurus* (see Selander and Giller, 1963) currently includes a number of species ranging from the United States to South America; most are distinguished by black and white barring on the back, although this is much reduced in some forms. *Melanerpes* includes the acorn woodpecker (*M. formicivorus*), found from Oregon to Colombia, the red-headed woodpecker (*M. erythrocephalus*) of the eastern United States, and two species endemic to West Indian islands; they have been characterized by solid patches of bright coloration and a lack of dorsal barring. Selander and Giller (op. cit.) did not lump *Melanerpes* and *Centurus*, but pointed out the similarity between *M. portoricensis* and *C. cruentatus* (a form which lacks dorsal barring), and the resemblance between the juvenile plumages of *M. erythrocephalus* and *Centurus* species. In addition, they considered the tropical genus *Tripsurus* congeneric with *Centurus*, as they were unable to find a character by which the two could be distinguished. Finally, the acorn woodpecker, which is unique in its social behavior, is placed by some workers in the monotypic genus *Balanosphyra*.

Asyndesmus appears more closely allied to those species currently placed in *Melanerpes*. It is remarkably similar in coloration to *M. herminieri* of Guadeloupe Island, which lacks the red face and silver collar of *Asyndesmus* but otherwise is similar in being all black except for a reddish breast and belly. Ecologically and behaviorally the Lewis woodpecker resembles the red-headed woodpecker (*M. erythrocephalus*), which, like *Asyndesmus*, (1) prefers open woods or burns for breeding habitat (Bent, 1939; Selander and Giller, 1959), (2) feeds extensively by flycatching (Bent, 1939), (3) maintains individually defended winter caches of acorns or beechnuts (Kilham, 1958b), (4) stores nuts in pieces in natural cavities (although unlike *Asyndesmus* it may seal them in with shredded bark; Hay, 1887; Kilham, 1958a), (5) excavates very little for wood-boring insects (Beal, 1911) and (6) is known to take large quantities of wild and cultivated fruit (Beal, op. cit.). Lewis and Clark (in Burroughs, 1961:240) noted upon their discovery of the Lewis woodpecker that "this bird in its actions when flying resembles the small red-headed woodpecker common to the Atlantic states; its note also somewhat resembles that bird."

The current American Ornithologists' Union Checklist (1957) places the red-headed and acorn woodpeckers in *Melanerpes,* but recognizes *Asyndesmus* as a monotypic genus. Although a revision of nomenclature is premature until the *Centurus-Melanerpes* problem is resolved, I feel strongly that *M. formicivorus* is *at least* as distinct from *M. erythrocephalus* as is *Asyndesmus.* While the acorn and red-headed woodpeckers perhaps are more similar in size and plumage (especially in possessing a white rump and wing bars), in a variety of other ways the Lewis and red-headed woodpeckers are much more alike (table 18). Therefore it

TABLE 18
COMPARISON AMONG THE LEWIS, RED-HEADED, AND ACORN WOODPECKERS

Characteristic	Lewis	Red-headed	Acorn
Adult plumage	monomorphic	monomorphic	dimorphic
Juvenile plumage	distinct	distinct	resembles adult
Breeding units	pairs	pairs	communal groups
Winter social groupings	individual territories	individual territories	colonies
Status	partially migratory	partially migratory	resident
Range	w. U. S.	e. U. S.	Oregon to Colombia
Store acorns	in pieces	in pieces	often unshelled and intact

seems appropriate, if *Asyndesmus* is retained, also to place the acorn woodpecker in its own genus, *Balanosphyra.* Another alternative would be to place all three species in *Melanerpes* and even to include *Centurus,* as Peters (1948) has done.

The behavioral and ecological similarity between *Asyndesmus* and *Melanerpes erythrocephalus,* and the fact that they have virtually complementary breeding ranges in the western and eastern United States, suggests a possible common ancestry. The red-headed woodpecker meets the Lewis in central Montana, and in eastern Wyoming, Colorado, and New Mexico. The only extensive range overlap occurs on the plains of eastern Colorado. I have found no published accounts of the two species actually breeding sympatrically, although this must certainly occur in Colorado. I am proposing here one means by which the evolution of these two woodpeckers *could* have taken place, assuming for the sake of speculation that such a differentiation *did* occur.

Recently, Short (1965) has attributed the origin of the eastern yellow-shafted (*Colaptes auratus*) and western red-shafted (*C. cafer*) flickers to a Pleistocene barrier caused by glacial ice in the north and formation of the arid plains in what is now the central United States during the Pliocene. Short (op. cit.) pointed out that the only suitable woodpecker habitat on these plains would have been the wooded areas along rivers, and cited evidence that during the Pliocene the drainage pattern was north-south rather than east-west as it is today (Frye and Leonard, 1952; Meneley et al., 1957). Since both forms of *Colaptes* today range north into the forests of western Canada, Short argued that the Pliocene aridity could not have resulted in separation of *C. auratus* and *C. cafer* until the Pleistocene glaciers caused completion of the barrier in the north.

Asyndesmus and *Melanerpes erythrocephalus* appear much more strongly differentiated than the two flickers. Other North American sibling species pairs such as buntings (*Passerina*), orioles (*Icterus*), and grosbeaks (*Pheucticus*) which meet on the Great Plains also show more similarity than the two woodpeckers in question (Sibley and Short, 1959; West, 1962; Sibley, 1964). Hybridization occurs between these pairs, particularly in the flickers which Short (1965) considers conspecific. In contrast, no hybrids are known between *Asyndesmus* and *M. erythrocephalus*. All of this points to an earlier and more prolonged separation between the Lewis and red-headed woodpeckers. The flickers, orioles, grosbeaks, and buntings all currently breed north into Canada, while along their zone of contact the Lewis and red-headed woodpeckers range only as far north as northern Montana. This means that the theoretical common ancestor could have been separated earlier than the other species into eastern and western populations solely by the formation of the southern plains during the Pliocene, before glaciation. This isolation may have lasted until development of the east-west drainage pattern brought the red-headed woodpecker across the plains as far as the Rocky Mountains, and into contact with the now distinct *Asyndesmus*.

Prior to the Pliocene formation of the Great Plains, much of North America was covered by a transcontinental "Arcto-Tertiary Flora" (Chaney, 1947), characterized by a mixture of broad-leafed deciduous and evergreen trees, and conifers, much as is found in the eastern United States today. Increasing aridity and cooling during the Miocene and Pliocene caused the formation of the central plains behind the rain shadow of the Rocky Mountains (Braun, 1947), separating this flora into eastern and western elements. In the west, reduction of summer rainfall resulted in restriction of the mesic Arcto-Tertiary Flora species to moister upland sites, and in the loss of broad-leafed elements (such as many of the eastern oaks). This resulted in the formation of the conifer-dominated forests common today in western mountains. At the same time the "sclerophyllous and microphyllous Madro-Tertiary Geoflora" (Axelrod, 1958:434), which had arisen in the drier southwestern North America in the Early Tertiary began to spread into lowland areas of the western United States. This flora includes many modern "chaparral" species in addition to the common scrub and live oaks.

The events just described suggest an intriguing possibility regarding the intense competition for acorns between the acorn woodpecker, which is restricted everywhere north of the tropics to Madro-Tertiary oak woodland, and the Lewis woodpecker, which seemingly is of Arcto-Tertiary origin. Assume that *Asyndesmus* (or progenitor) at one time was resident in the broad-leafed oak woodlands of western North America. This is essentially the situation for the red-headed woodpecker today throughout much of its range in the east. As the western Arcto-Tertiary Flora lost its oaks, the ancestral Lewis woodpecker would have been forced to move to the xeric oak woodlands of the invading Madro-Tertiary Flora. Here it would have encountered the acorn woodpecker—a species equally if not better adapted to harvest and utilize mast. Thus this competitive situation may be the result of parallel evolution in different floristic regions. The ancestral *Asyndesmus* population may have evolved its opportunistic habits, as well as its specializations for flycatching, under selection pressure resulting from interspecific competition.

SUMMARY

1. The Lewis woodpecker (*Asyndesmus lewis*) is found regularly from eastern Colorado west to the Pacific, and from British Columbia to northernmost Mexico. The details of its distribution relate to seasonal food requirements. During the breeding season it feeds largely by hawking insects, and thus prefers open habitat with a good source of free-living insects—yellow pine forest or old burns at higher elevations, riparian cottonwood or sycamore groves in the lowlands. In winter Lewis woodpeckers rely heavily upon stored mast, usually acorns or some agricultural equivalent such as almonds and walnuts.

2. *Asyndesmus lewis* is basically an opportunistic species, concentrating in areas where food happens to be abundant. In April or May birds move to areas with numerous free-living insects; in August or September they return to oaks or orchards rich in mast. If a particular area supports sufficient amounts of both then they may be permanently resident. Because of their opportunism, Lewis woodpeckers are sporadic in occurrence, moving into an area in large numbers one year and being totally absent the next.

3. *Asyndesmus* shows adaptations for capturing flying rather than wood-boring insects in having broader wings with a lighter load, smaller legs, and a skull less specialized to absorb hard blows and capable of a greater gape than other North American woodpeckers. Perhaps related to their opportunistic feeding behavior, there is no apparent difference between the sexes in foraging techniques.

4. Lewis woodpeckers in California never were seen excavating for sub-surface insects. In the breeding season they spent 57.9 percent of their foraging time in flycatching, 32.1 percent feeding on free-living insects taken off the ground or in brush, and 10.0 percent gleaning the surfaces of live and dead trees. In winter they spent 71.5 percent harvesting, storing, and utilizing acorns or almonds, 15.2 percent flycatching, and 13.3 percent gleaning. Time spent in food-related activities varied during the winter. In October and November Lewis woodpeckers were busy in the accumulation of acorns or almonds. During January, February, and early March, activity was low due to the large and readily available food cache. In late March and April birds became active again as their mast stores became depleted; they turned largely to flycatching and gleaning. A study of birds wintering in almond groves where mast was superabundant indicated that Lewis woodpeckers store as many nuts as possible without regard for the number accumulated. Acorn availability is such that selection apparently has favored the individual which stored as much mast as possible.

5. Each individual Lewis woodpecker (or rarely a pair) harvests, accumulates, and defends its own acorn cache. There is no winter territory except the storage site, but this is vigorously protected both inter- and intraspecifically. By recording the number of interactions between a resident individual and all other birds per unit time it was possible to obtain a direct index of the intensity of competition between *Asyndesmus* and various bird species. This is of interest because competition usually is studied only indirectly.

6. The Lewis woodpecker competes in California with the acorn woodpecker (*Melanerpes formicivorus*), a species which occurs in oak woodland and which

also accumulates acorns in the fall. Since the acorn woodpecker is abundant in California, the scarcer Lewis woodpecker probably coexists by reason of its opportunism, and may be a "fugitive species" (Hutchinson, 1951).

7. Rates of aggressive interaction related to cache defense were highest in January and February, when the birds had the largest amounts of mast stored. This shows that the food cache is the focal point of the competition observed. Interaction rates were generally higher in winter than during the breeding season. This does not necessarily mean that food was more scarce in winter, but its accumulation in one place apparently attracts interspecific competitors. In winter the number of interspecific encounters greatly exceeded intraspecific conflicts, suggesting that, from the point of view of a Lewis woodpecker defending its store, interspecific competition was the more important. The mast store represents such a readily available and concentrated energy source that a large number of species become potential competitors, often to the point where they constitute a greater threat than other *Asyndesmus* simply because of their collective abundance.

8. Lewis woodpeckers apparently mate for life, or at least show a marked nest fidelity. They breed significantly earlier in lowlands than in the mountains; timing of nesting in the Sierra Nevada depended upon local weather conditions—another manifestation of their opportunism. There is no breeding territory save that of the nest site, nesting pairs often feeding semi-gregariously where insects happen to be temporarily abundant. Incubation lasted about two weeks, with the male being more attentive during the day and incubating alone at night. Fledging lasted about a month. Adults fed an average of 15 times per hour; they showed no obvious variation with time of day or age of the nestlings. Males slept with young, but the sexes shared diurnal nest duties. Juveniles retain the drab body plumage until they leave the adults in the fall and establish their own acorn stores. This suggests that retention of the duller plumage has evolved as a means of reducing aggression between young and their parents.

9. *Asyndesmus* appears related to the genus *Melanerpes*. It is particularly similar in ecology and behavior to the red-headed woodpecker (*M. erythrocephalus*). This resemblance, in addition to closely complementary breeding ranges in the eastern and western United States, suggests a common ancestry. A possible means of this evolution is suggested, based upon the formation of arid plains in central North America during the Pliocene. The intense competition seen today between the Lewis and acorn woodpeckers may be the result of parallel evolution of the former in the western Arcto-Tertiary Geoflora and the latter in the Madro-Tertiary Geoflora, followed by sympatry when *Asyndesmus* was forced to move due to the extinction of oaks in its normal habitat.

LITERATURE CITED

ADAMS, L.
- 1941. Lewis woodpecker migration. Condor, 43:119.

ALDERSON, V. A.
- 1890. Hairy woodpecker and potato bugs. Oologist, 7:147.

AMERICAN ORNITHOLOGISTS' UNION
- 1957. Checklist of North American birds (5th ed.) Publ. by A. O. U.

AXELROD, D. I.
- 1958. Evolution of the Madro-Tertiary Geoflora. Bot. Rev., 24:433–509.

BAILEY, A. M., and R. J. NIEDRACH
- 1965. The birds of Colorado. Denver: Denver Mus. Natur. Hist.

BAILEY, F. M.
- 1928. Birds of New Mexico. New Mexico Department of Fish and Game.

BAIRD, S. F., T. M. BREWER, and R. RIDGWAY
- 1875. A history of North American birds, vol. II. Boston: Little, Brown, and Co.

BALDWIN, P. H., and R. W. SCHNEIDER
- 1963. Flight in relation to form of wing in the Lewis' Woodpecker. J. Colo.-Wyo. Acad. Sci., 5:58–59.

BEAL, F. E. L.
- 1911. Food of the woodpeckers of the United States. U. S. Dept. Agric. Biol. Surv., Bull. no. 37.

BEHLE, W. H.
- 1943. Birds of the Pine Valley Mountain region, southwestern Utah. Bull. Univ. Utah, 34:1–85.
- 1955. The birds of the Deep Creek Mountains of central western Utah. Univ. Utah Biol. Ser. 11:1–34.
- 1958. The birds of the Raft River Mountains, northwestern Utah. Univ. Utah Biol. Ser. 11:1–40.

BELDING, L.
- 1878. A partial list of the birds of central California. Proc. U. S. Nat. Mus., 1:388–449.
- 1890. Land birds of the Pacific District. San Francisco: California Academy of Sciences.
- 1901. May in the high Sierras. Condor, 3:31.

BENDIRE, C.
- 1895. Life histories of North American birds. U. S. Nat. Mus., Spec. Bull. No. 3.

BENT, A. C.
- 1939. Life histories of North American woodpeckers. U. S. Nat. Mus., Bull. 174:1–334.

BIRCH, L. C.
- 1957. The meanings of competition. Amer. Natur., 91:5–18.

BLACKFORD, J. L.
- 1955. Woodpecker concentration in burned forest. Condor, 57:28–30.

BLINCOE, B. J.
- 1923. Random notes on the feeding habits of some Kentucky birds. Wilson Bull., 35:63–71.

BOCK, W.
- 1963. Evolution and phylogeny in morphologically uniform groups. Amer. Natur., 97:265–285.
- 1966. An approach to the functional analysis of bill shape. Auk, 83:10–51.

———, and W. DEW. MILLER
- 1959. The scansorial foot of woodpeckers, with comments on the evolution of perching and climbing feet in birds. Amer. Mus. Novitates, 1931:1–45.

BOLANDER, L. P.
- 1930. Is the Lewis woodpecker a regular breeder in the San Francisco region? Condor, 32:263–4.

BRAUN, E. L.
- 1947. Development of the deciduous forests of eastern North America. Ecol. Monogr., 17:211–219.

BREWSTER, W.
  1898. Lewis's woodpecker storing acorns. Auk, 15:188.
BROOKS, A.
  1917. Birds of the Chilliwack district, British Columbia. Auk, 34:28–50.
BROOKS, M.
  1934. An unusual woodpecker accident. Auk, 51:379.
BROWN, H.
  1902. An unusual abundance of Lewis' woodpeckers near Tucson, Arizona. Auk, 19:80–83.
BROWN, J. L.
  1964. The evolution of diversity in avian territorial systems. Wilson Bull., 76:160–169.
BRUNER, L., R. H. WALCOTT, and M. H. SWENK
  1904. A preliminary review of the birds of Nebraska. Omaha.
BRYANT, H. C.
  1921. California woodpecker steals eggs of wood pewee. Condor, 23:33.
BURLEIGH, T. D.
  1921. Breeding birds of Warland, Lincoln County, Montana. Auk, 38:552–565.
BURROUGHS, R. D.
  1961. The natural history of the Lewis and Clark expedition. East Lansing: Michigan State University Press.
BURT, W. H.
  1929. Pterylography of certain North American woodpeckers. Univ. Calif. Publ. Zool., 30:427–442.
  1930. Adaptive modifications in the woodpeckers. Univ. Calif. Publ. Zool., 32:455–524.
CHANEY, R. W.
  1947. Tertiary centers and migration routes. Ecol. Monogr. 17:139–148.
CHAPMAN, F. M.
  1890. On a collection of birds made by Mr. Clark P. Streator in British Columbia, with field notes by the collector. Bull. Amer. Mus. Natur. Hist., 3:123–158.
CLARK, E. C.
  1956. The Great Basin tent caterpillar in relation to bitterbrush in California. Calif. Fish and Game, 42:131–142.
COOPER, J. G.
  1870. Ornithology of California, Vol. I. Land birds. Cambridge: University Press (Welch, Bigelow, and Co.).
  ———, and G. SUCKLEY
  1859. The natural history of Washington Territory. New York: Bailliere Bros.
COUES, E.
  1874. Birds of the Northwest. U. S. Geol. Surv. of the Territories: Misc. Publ. no. 3.
COWAN, I. McT.
  1940. Winter occurrence of summer birds on Vancouver Island, British Columbia. Condor, 42:213–14.
CROWELL, K. L.
  1962. Reduced interspecific competition among birds of Bermuda. Ecology, 43:75–88.
CURRIER, E. S.
  1928. Lewis woodpeckers nesting in colonies. Condor, 30:356.
DALE, R. F.
  1959. Climates of the states—California. Washington: U. S. Department of Commerce.
DARLINGTON, P. J.
  1957. Zoogeography. New York: J. Wiley.
DARWIN, C.
  1859. On the origin of species. London.
DAVIS, J.
  1965. Natural history, variation, and distribution of the Strickland's woodpecker. Auk, 82:537–90.
  ———, G. F. FISLER, and B. S. DAVIS
  1963. The breeding biology of the western flycatcher. Condor, 65:337–382.

Dawson, W. L.
  1897. A preliminary list of the birds of Okanagan County, Washington. Auk, 14:168–182.
  ———, and J. H. Bowles
  1909. The birds of Washington. Seattle: The Occidental Publishing Co.
DeBach, P.
  1966. The competitive displacement and coexistence principles. Annu. Rev. Entomol., 11:183–212.
Dice, L. R.
  1921. A bird census at Prescott, Walla Walla County, Washington. Condor, 23:87–90.
Dicks, F.
  1932. A word on the bird life at Maplewood Springs. Murrelet, 13:23.
Drew, F. M.
  1881. Field notes on the birds of San Juan County, Colorado. Auk, 6:138–143.
Elton, C.
  1946. Competition and the structure of ecological communities. J. Anim. Ecol., 15:54–68.
Farner, D. S.
  1952. The birds of Crater Lake National Park. Lawrence: Univ. Kansas Press.
Ferry, J. F.
  1908. Notes from the diary of a naturalist in northern California. Condor, 10:30–44.
Fisher, A. K.
  1893. Birds of the Death Valley expedition. North American Fauna no. 7.
Frye, J. C., and A. B. Leonard
  1952. Pleistocene geology of Kansas. Univ. Kan., State Geol. Surv. Kansas, Bull. no. 99, p. 1–230.
Gabrielson, I. N., and S. G. Jewett
  1940. Birds of Oregon. Corvallis: Oregon State College.
Garrod, A. H.
  1873. On certain muscles of the thigh of birds and their value in classification. Proc. Zool. Soc. London, 1873:626–644.
Gause, G. F.
  1934. The struggle for existence. Baltimore: Williams and Wilkins.
Gilman, M. F.
  1907. Some birds of southwest Colorado. Condor, 9:152–158.
  1936. Additional bird records from Death Valley. Condor, 38:40–41.
Gladding, H. M.
  1942. Nests in the cottonwoods at Gustine, California. Condor, 44:226.
Greenwalt, C. H.
  1962. Dimensional relationships for flying animals. Smithsonian Misc. Publ. 144:1–46.
Grinnell, J.
  1928. The presence and absence of animals. Univ. Calif. Chron., 30:429–450.
  ———, J. Dixon, and J. M. Linsdale
  1930. Vertebrate natural history of a section of northern California, through the Lassen Peak region. Univ. Calif. Publ. Zool., 35:1–594.
  ———, and C. Lamb
  1927. New bird records from Lower California. Condor, 29:124–26.
  ———, and T. I. Storer
  1924. Animal Life in the Yosemite. Berkeley: Univ. California Press.
Hand, R. L.
  1941. Birds of the St. Joe National Forest. Condor, 43:220–232.
Hardin, G.
  1960. The competitive exclusion principle. Science, 131:1292–1298.
Harrington, H. D.
  1964. Manual of the plants of Colorado. Denver: Sage Books.
Hay, O. P.
  1887. The red-headed woodpecker a hoarder. Auk, 4:193–196.

HELME, A. H.
    1882. Red-headed woodpeckers. Ornithol. and Oologist, 7:107.
HENSHAW, H. W.
    1875. Report on the ornithological collections. In G. M. Wheeler: Report upon the geographical and geological surveys west of the 100th meridian. Washington: U. S. Gov't. Press.
HINDE, R. A.
    1966. Animal Behaviour. New York: McGraw-Hill Book Co.
HITCHCOCK, C. L., A. CRONQUIST, M. OWNBEY, and J. W. THOMPSON
    1964. Vascular plants of the Pacific Northwest. Seattle: Univ. Wash. Press.
HOFFMANN, R.
    1927. The Lewis woodpecker apparently nesting at Gustine, Merced County, California. Condor, 29:165.
HUBBARD, D. H.
    1941. Vertebrate animals of the Friant Reservoir Basin. Calif. Fish and Game, 27:198–215.
HUEY, C. M.
    1931. Two new birds and other records for Lower California. Condor, 33:127–128.
HUNN, J. T. S.
    1906. Notes on birds of Silver City, New Mexico. Auk, 23:418–425.
HUTCHINSON, G. E.
    1951. Copepodology for the ornithologist. Ecology, 32:571–577.
JENSEN, J. K.
    1923. Notes on the nesting birds of northern Santa Fe County, New Mexico. Auk, 40:452–469.
JEPSON, W. L.
    1911. A flora of western middle California (2nd ed.). San Francisco: Cunningham, Curtiss and Welch.
JEWETT, S. G.
    1909. Some birds of Baker County, Oregon. Auk, 26:5–9.
———, and I. N. GABRIELSON
    1929. Birds of the Portland area, Oregon, Pacific Coast Avifauna no. 19.
———, W. P. TAYLOR, W. T. SHAW, and J. W. ALDRICH
    1953. Birds of Washington State. Seattle: Univ. Washington Press.
JOHNSON, D. H., M. D. BRYANT, and A. H. MILLER
    1948. Vertebrate animals of the Providence Mountains area of California. Univ. Calif. Publ. Zool., 48:221–375.
JOHNSON, N. K.
    Birds of western Nevada (unpublished manuscript).
JOHNSTON, R. F.
    1960. Directory to the bird-life of Kansas. Univ. Kans. Mus. Natur. Hist., Misc. Publ. no. 23, p. 1–61.
JOHNSTONE, W. B.
    1949. The birds of the East Kootenay. Occas. Pap. Brit. Columbia Prov. Mus. no. 7.
KEARNEY, T. H., and R. H. PEEBLES
    1960. Arizona flora. Second edition with a supplement by J. T. Howell and E. McClintock. Berkeley and Los Angeles: Univ. Calif. Press.
KENDEIGH, S. C.
    1952. Parental care and its evolution in birds. Illinois Biol. Monogr., vol. 22, nos. 1–3.
KILHAM, L.
    1958a. Sealed-in winter stores of red-headed woodpeckers. Wilson Bull., 70:107–113.
    1958b. Territorial behavior of wintering red-headed woodpeckers. Wilson Bull., 70:347–358.
    1958c. Pair formation, mutual tapping, and nest-hole selection of red-bellied woodpeckers. Auk, 75:318–339.
    1959a. Early reproductive behavior of flickers. Wilson Bull., 71:323.
    1959b. Behavior and methods of communication of pileated woodpeckers. Condor, 61:377–387.
    1960. Courtship and territorial behavior of the hairy woodpecker. Auk, 77:259–270.

1961. Reproductive behavior of red-bellied woodpeckers. Wilson Bull., 73:237–254.
1962. Breeding behavior of yellow-bellied sapsuckers. Auk, 79:31–43.
1963. Food storing of red-bellied woodpeckers. Wilson Bull., 75:227–234.
1965. Differences in feeding behavior of male and female hairy woodpeckers. Wilson Bull., 77:134–145.

KITCHIN, E. A.
1949. Birds of the Olympic Peninsula. Port Angeles, Washington: Olympic Stationers.

KNIGHT, W. C.
1902. The birds of Wyoming. Wyo. Exp. Sta. Bull. No. 55.

LAMB, C.
1912. Birds of a Mojave Desert oasis. Condor, 14:32–40.

LAMB, C., and A. B. HOWELL
1913. Notes from Buena Vista Lake and Fort Tejon. Condor, 15:115–120.

LANYON, W. E.
1957. The comparative biology of the meadowlarks (*Sturnella*) in Wisconsin. Publications Nuttall Ornithol. Club, no. 1.

LAW, J. E.
1929. Another Lewis woodpecker stores acorns. Condor, 31:233–238.

LAWRENCE, L. DE K.
1967. A comparative life-history study of four species of woodpeckers. Ornithol. Monogr. no. 5, p. 1–156. Publ. by The American Ornithologists' Union.

LEACH, F. A.
1925. Communism in the California woodpecker. Condor, 27:12–19.

LIGON, J. D.
1968. Observations on Strickland's woodpecker, *Dendrocopos stricklandi*. Condor, 70:83–4.

LIGON, J. S.
1961. New Mexico birds and where to find them. Albuquerque: Univ. New Mexico Press.

LINSDALE, J. M.
1936a. The birds of Nevada. Pacfic Coast Avifauna no. 23.
1936b. Habits of Lewis woodpeckers in winter. Condor, 38:245–246.
1946. The California ground squirrel. Berkeley and Los Angeles: Univ. Calif. Press.

LOTKA, A. J.
1925. Elements of physical biology. Baltimore: Williams and Wilkins.

MACARTHUR, R. H.
1957. On the relative abundance of bird species. Proc. Nat. Acad. Sci., 43:293–295.
1958. Population ecology of some warblers of northeastern coniferous forests. Ecology, 39:599–619.
1960. On the relative abundance of species. Amer. Natur., 94:26–35.

MARSDEN, H. W.
1907. Feeding habits of the Lewis woodpecker. Condor, 9:27.

MAYR, E.
1963. Animal species and evolution. Cambridge: The Belknap Press of Harvard University Press.

MENELEY, W. A., E. A. CHRISTIANSEN, and W. O. KUPSCH
1957. Preglacial Missouri River in Saskatchewan. J. Geol., 65:441–447.

MERRIAM, C. H.
1890. Results of a biological survey of the San Francisco Mountains region and desert of the Little Colorado, Arizona. North American Fauna no. 3.
1891. Results of a biological reconnaissance of south-central Idaho. North American Fauna no. 5.

MERRILL, J. C.
1888. Notes on the birds of Fort Klamath, Oregon. Auk, 5:251–262.

MICHAEL, C. W.
1926. Acorn storing methods of the California and Lewis woodpeckers. Condor, 28:68.

MICHAEL, E.
  1932. Feeding habits of woodpeckers in the Yosemite Valley. Yosemite Nature Notes, 11:3–4.
MILLER, A.H., H. FRIEDMANN, L. GRISCOM, and R. T. MOORE
  1957. Distributional check-list of the birds of Mexico, part II. Pacific Coast Avifauna no. 33
———, and R. C. STEBBINS
  1964. The lives of desert animals in Joshua Tree National Monument. Berkeley and Los Angeles: Univ. Calif. Press.
MILLER, L. H.
  1904. The birds of the John Day region, Oregon. Condor, 6:100–106.
MILNE, A.
  1961. Definition of competition among animals. Soc. Exp. Biol. Symp. no. 15, p. 40–61.
MOREAU, R. E.
  1948. Ecological isolation in a rich tropical avifauna. J. Anim. Ecol., 17:113–126.
MUNRO, J. A.
  1930. Miscellaneous notes on some British Columbia birds. Condor, 32:65–68.
———, and I. McT. COWAN
  1947. A review of the bird fauna of British Columbia. Brit. Columbia Provincial Mus., Spec. Publ. no. 2.
MUNZ, P. A.
  1959. A California flora. Berkeley and Los Angeles: Univ. Calif. Press.
NEFF, J. A.
  1928. A study of the economic status of the common woodpeckers in relation to Oregon horticulture. Marionville, Missouri: Free Press Print.
  1947. Habits, food, and economic status of the band-tailed pigeon. North American Fauna no. 58.
NEWBERRY, J. S.
  1857. Pacific Railroad Surveys, vol. 6. Report upon the birds, p. 73–110.
NICE, M. M.
  1941. The role of territory in bird life. Amer. Midland Natur., 26:441–487.
NICHOLSON, A. J.
  1933. The balance of animal populations. J. Anim. Ecol., 2:131–178.
NUTTALL, T.
  1840. Manual of the ornithology of the United States and of Canada (2nd ed.) Boston: Hilliard, Gray, and Co.
OBERHOLSER, H. C.
  1927. The migration of North American birds. XXXV. Red-headed and Lewis's woodpeckers. Bird Lore, 29:411–413.
ODUM, E. P.
  1959. Fundamentals of ecology (2nd ed.). Philadelphia: W. B. Saunders Co.
ORIANS, G. H., and G. COLLIER
  1963. Competition and blackbird social systems. Evolution, 17:449–459.
PEARSE, T.
  1946. Notes on changes in bird populations in the vicinity of Comox, Vancouver Island. Murrelet, 27:4–9.
PEATTIE, D. C.
  1953. A natural history of western trees. Boston: Houghton Mifflin Company.
PECK, M. E.
  1911. Summer birds of Willow Creek, Malheur County, Oregon. Condor, 13:63–69.
  1961. A manual of the higher plants of Oregon (2nd ed.). Portland: Binsford and Mort.
PETERS, J. L.
  1948. Check-list of birds of the world. Volume VI–Piciformes. Cambridge: Harvard Univ. Press.
PETTINGILL, O. S., JR., and N. R. WHITNEY, JR.
  1965. Birds of the Black Hills. Spec. Publ. no. 1, Cornell Lab. Ornithol.

PHILLIPS, A. R., J. T. MARSHALL, and G. MONSON
  1964. The birds of Arizona. Tucson: Univ. Arizona Press.
PITELKA, F. A.
  1951. Ecologic overlap and interspecific strife in breeding populations of Anna and Allen hummingbirds. Ecology, 32:641–661.
RAMP, W.
  1965. The auditory range of a hairy woodpecker. Condor, 67:183–185.
RATHBUN, S. F.
  1902. A list of the land birds of Seattle, Washington, and vicinity. Auk, 19:131–141.
REED, A. D.
  1966. An analysis of almond production costs in California. Davis: Univ. Calif. Agric. Extension Service.
RHOADS, S. N.
  1893. The birds observed in British Columbia and Washington during the spring and summer, 1892. Proc. Nat. Acad. Sci. Philadelphia, 45:21–65.
RIDGWAY, R.
  1874. Lists of birds observed at various localities contiguous to the Central Pacific Railroad, from Sacramento City, California, to Salt Lake City, Utah. Bull. Essex Institute, 6:169–174.
RITTER, W. E.
  1938. The California woodpecker and I. Berkeley: Univ. Calif. Press.
ROBERTSON, J. McB.
  1935. Lewis woodpecker in Death Valley. Condor, 37:173.
ROCKWELL, R. B.
  1908. An annotated list of the birds of Mesa County, Colorado. Condor, 10:152–180.
  ———, and A. WETMORE
  1914. A list of birds from the vicinity of Golden, Colorado. Auk, 31:309–333.
ROOT, R. B.
  1966. The avian response to a population outbreak of a tent caterpillar, *Malacosoma constrictum* (Stretch). Pan-Pacific Entomol., 42:48–53.
  1967. The niche exploitation pattern of the blue-gray gnatcatcher. Ecol. Monogr., 37:317–350.
SAUNDERS, A. A.
  1911. A preliminary list of the birds of Gallatin County, Montana. Auk, 28:26–49.
  1914. The birds of Teton and northern Lewis and Clark counties, Montana. Condor, 16:124–144.
  1921. A distributional list of the birds of Montana. Pacific Coast Avifauna no. 14.
SAVILE, D. B. O.
  1957. Adaptive evolution in the avian wing. Evolution, 11:212–224.
SCLATER, W. L.
  1912. A history of the birds of Colorado. London: Witherby and Company.
SCOTT, W. E. D.
  1886. On the avifauna of Pinal County, with remarks on some birds of Pima and Gila counties, Arizona. Auk, 8:421–432.
SELANDER, R. K.
  1966. Sexual dimorphism and differential niche utilization in birds. Condor, 68:113–151.
  ———, and D. R. GILLER
  1959. Interspecific relationships of woodpeckers in Texas. Wilson Bull., 71:107–124.
  ———, and D. R. GILLER
  1963. Species limits in the woodpecker genus *Centurus*. Bull. Amer. Mus. Natur. Hist., 124 (art. 6):215–273.
SHELDON, H. H.
  1907. A collecting trip by wagon to Eagle Lake, Sierra Nevada mountains. Condor, 9:185–191.
SHERWOOD, W. E.
  1927. Feeding habits of Lewis woodpecker. Condor, 29:171.

SHORT, L. L., JR.
  1965. Hybridization in the flickers (*Colaptes*) of North America. Bull. Amer. Mus. Natur. Hist., 129, article 4.
SIBLEY, C. G.
  1964. Hybridization in the orioles of the Great Plains. Condor, 66:130–150.
———, and L. L. SHORT, JR.
  1959. Hybridization in the buntings (*Passerina*) of the Great Plains. Auk, 76:443–463.
SILLOWAY, P. M.
  1901. Summer birds of Flathead Lake. Bull. Univ. Montana no. 1.
SLOBODKIN, L. B.
  1964. Growth and regulation of animal populations. New York: Holt, Rinehart, and Winston.
SMITH, C. F.
  1941. Lewis woodpecker migration. Condor, 43:76.
SNODGRASS, R. E.
  1903. A list of land birds from central Washington. Auk, 20:202–209.
  1904. A list of land birds from central and southeastern Washington. Auk, 21:223–233.
SNOW, R. B.
  1940. A natural history of the Lewis woodpecker, *Asyndesmus lewis* (Gray). M. A. Thesis, Univ. of Utah.
SOUTHERN, W. E.
  1960. Copulatory behavior of *Melanerpes erythrocephalus*. Auk, 77:218–219.
SPRING, L. W.
  1965. Climbing and perching adaptations in some North American woodpeckers. Condor, 67:457–488.
STICKEL, D. W.
  1965. Territorial and breeding habits of red-bellied woodpeckers. Amer. Midland Natur., 74:110–118.
STREATOR, C. P.
  1886. List of birds observed in the vicinity of Santa Barbara, California, during the year 1885. Ornithol. and Oologist, 11:66–67.
SWENK, J. B., F. W. HAECKER, and R. A. MOSER
  1945. Check-list of birds of Nebraska. Nebr. Bird Rev., 13:1–44.
TAVERNER, P. A.
  1926. Birds of western Canada. Victoria Memorial Mus., Bull. no. 41, Biol. Ser. 10:1–380.
THOMPSON, C. S.
  1900. The woodpeckers of the Upper Salinas Valley. Condor, 2:52–55.
TINBERGEN, N.
  1952. Derived activities: their causation, biological significance, origin and emancipation during evolution. Quart. Rev. Biol., 27:1–32.
TODD, W. E. C.
  1946. Critical notes on the woodpeckers. Ann. Carnegie Mus., 30 (art. 17):297–317.
TOUT, W.
  1947. Lincoln County birds. North Platte, Nebraska: The Author.
TOWNSEND, C. H.
  1887. Field notes on the mammals, birds, and reptiles of northern California. Proc. U. S. Nat. Mus., 10:159–241.
UDVARDY, M. D. F.
  1959. Notes on the ecological concepts of habitat, biotype, and niche. Ecology, 40:725–728.
VAN TYNE, J.
  1926. An unusual flight of arctic three-toed woodpeckers. Auk, 43:469–474.
VAURIE, C.
  1951. Adaptive differences between two sympatric species of nuthatches (*Sitta*). Proc. X Int. Ornithol. Congr., 1950:163–166.

VOLTERRA, V.
  1926. Variazoni e fluttuazoni del numero d'individui in specie animali convivanti. Mem. accad. Lincei, (6)2:31–113.
WALKER, A.
  1917. Some birds of central Oregon. Condor, 19:131–140.
  1924. Notes on some birds from Tillamook County, Oregon. Condor, 26:180–182.
WARREN, E. R.
  1916. Notes on the birds of the Elk Mountain region, Gunnison County, Colorado. Auk, 33:292–317.
WEAVER, J. E.
  1965. Native vegetation of Nebraska. Lincoln: Univ. Nebr. Press.
WELCH, J. M.
  1899. Notes on Lewis's woodpecker. Condor, 1:29.
WEST, D. A.
  1962. Hybridization in grosbeaks (*Pheucticus*) of the Great Plains. Auk, 79:399–424.
WEYDEMEYER, W., and D. WEYDEMEYER
  1928. The woodpeckers of Lincoln County, Montana. Condor, 30:339–346.
WILLIAMS, J. J.
  1905. Notes on the Lewis woodpecker. Condor, 7:56.
WILSON, A.
  1831. American ornithology. Edinburgh: Constable and Company.
WITHERBY, H. F., F. D. R. JOURDAIN, N. F. TICHEHURST, and B. W. TUCKER
  1943. The handbook of British birds. London: H. F. and G. Witherby, Ltd.
WOODBURY, A. M., C. COTTAM, and J. W. SNYDER
  1949. Annotated checklist of the birds of Utah. Bull. Univ. Utah, 39:1–40.
———, and H. N. RUSSELL, JR.
  1945. Birds of the Navahoe country. Bull. Univ. Utah, 35:1–157.
WRIGHT, H. W.
  1908. A death struggle. Condor, 10:93.
WYNNE-EDWARDS, V. C.
  1962. Animal dispersion in relation to social behavior. New York: Hafner Publishing Co.
YOCOM, C. F.
  1945. Summer birds of the Colville Valley and the Selkirk Mountains of Washington. Murrelet, 26:19–23.

PLATES

a. Lewis woodpecker breeding habitat—open ponderosa pine forest. Photographed in August, 1967, near Boca Reservoir, Nevada County, California.

b. Nest site in a dead ponderosa pine near Boca Reservoir. Photographed in August, 1967.

a. Lewis woodpecker breeding habitat—old burned coniferous forest. Photograph taken in July, 1965, of a hillside above Boca Reservoir which burned in 1946.

b. A coniferous forest burned too recently to be suitable Lewis woodpecker breeding habitat. Photograph taken in July, 1966, of a six year old burn near Sagehen Creek, Nevada County, California.

a. A burn too old to be suitable Lewis woodpecker breeding habitat. Photograph taken in September, 1965, of a burn near Sagehen Creek, Nevada County, California.

b. Lewis woodpecker breeding habitat—open cottonwood grove. Photograph taken May, 1967, of Fremont cottonwoods near Genoa, Douglas County, Nevada.

a. Lewis woodpecker breeding habitat—oak savannah. Photograph taken in April, 1967, of the San Antonio Valley, Santa Clara County, California.

b. Partially dead oak used as a nest site by a pair of Lewis woodpeckers. Photograph taken June, 1965, on the Old River, San Joaquin County, California.

a. Almond orchard visited by Lewis woodpeckers breeding near Livermore, Alameda County, California. Photograph taken in July, 1966.

b. Lewis woodpecker winter habitat—oak woodland. Photograph taken in March, 1967. The dead stub was used by a bird as a storage site, the large living tree serving as its roost.

a. Lewis woodpecker winter habitat—almond orchards. Photograph taken in November, 1967, in the Capay Valley, Solano County, California. Birds used the power poles as storage sites.

b. Power pole with desiccation cracks filled with almond meats placed there by a Lewis woodpecker. Photograph taken in November, 1967, in the Capay Valley.